Kleine Bauten
Small Structures

Edition Topos

Birkhäuser
Basel · Boston · Berlin

Topos
EUROPEAN
LANDSCAPE
MAGAZINE

Cover Photo:
Eckhart Matthäus

The renaissance of the folly: 25 red structures form the famous grid in the Parc de la Villette. Page 6

In the former moors near Groningen an Observatorium, an art object designed by the group Observatorium, serves cyclists and hikers as a place to rest and enjoy the view. Page 21

A footpath connects six green structures made up of trees and shrubs in Parco di Casvegno in Mendrisio. Page 37

On the occasion of Bruges' designation as the European Cultural Capital 2002, Toyo Ito built a temporary pavilion. Page 47

A public convenience in San Sebastián, Spain, reminds one of a reflecting monolith towering from the Basque rock. Page 58

Like a parasite, a small, garish green construction sits on a former factory building in Rotterdam. Page 52

A look-out in Souru, Finland, houses a sound installation recalling the daily life in a former workers' village. Page 79

*T*alked into going for a walk in the woods or over the fields, most children will whine. Usually the only thing that helps is having a goal, such as an observation tower or, better still, a kiosk where you can buy lemonade or ice cream. And the grown-ups? They are hardly any different: they may claim that the path is the goal, nature is so beautiful, being outdoors so healthy, the horizon so broad ... in the end, the fun for everyone, with the possible exception of people on desert hikes or expeditions and philosophers, culminates in a little hut somewhere. That is what lends the landscape a meaning and your exercise a point. When walking was still an alternative to driving cars, refuges and inns were essential. They provided rest and quiet, pleasures for the eyes, palate and stomach, and entertaining conversation. Forest café, grotto, rifugio are the promisingly connotative names of small buildings with great appeal. Even to a driver, of course, though you would be willing to admit that driving reduces the enjoyment. It makes the experience of space and time fundamentally different. While the days of highway robbers are over, the unconscious feeling of having reached a place of shelter does not arise if you arrive snugly ensconced in a moving cabin.

Do we feel comfortable over a longer period of time in a completely empty landscape without any architecture? Perhaps only once we have set up the portable goal we dragged along. Camping, on the ground or in a camper, is still closely related to the search for shelter in a cave or under a canopy of dense foliage. This may be why parks and landscapes only become acceptable and even beautiful through architecture, as demonstrated by the history of park design. Monopteros, temple of Diana, hermit's cave, Chinese Tower, fake ruins, folly and belvedere – these are all structures that enhance a place and make us aware of it. They once had a certain meaning and perhaps still have, even when you cannot buy hot dogs there.

In cities you usually notice the bigger buildings first. Then you take a closer look and see the small structures. They are often what constitute the charm or the special character of a street or a square. They appeal to us because we encounter them at eye level, as it were. They belong to the daily life of the city and thus to us. A refreshment stall, a newspaper stand, a tea pavilion, even public urinals, as well as transformer boxes, telephone booths reduced to poles and cupolas, bus stops, flower stalls, roast chestnut vendors' huts – a variety that creates an urban grid, not unlike Tschumi's follies in La Villette in that respect, albeit loosely associated. These small structures, whether mobile like a vegetable stall or solid like an advertising pillar, are what populate open spaces and, ideally, enhance them. They are the crystallisation points of social life.

Die meisten Kinder quengeln, überredet man sie zu einem Spaziergang in Wald und Flur. Abhilfe schafft meist nur ein Ziel, ein Aussichtsturm etwa, aber viel lieber noch ein Kiosk, in dem man Limonade kaufen kann oder ein Eis. Und die Erwachsenen? Verhalten sich kaum anders: Sie geben zwar vor, der Weg sei das Ziel, die Natur so schön, der Aufenthalt im Freien so gesund, der Horizont so weit ... Der Spaß kulminiert dann doch – Wüstenwanderer und Expeditionsteilnehmer sowie Philosophen vielleicht ausgenommen – wenn irgendwo ein klein' Hüttchen steht. Dies gibt dann der Landschaft Bedeutung und der eigenen Bewegung einen Sinn. Als das Gehen noch als Alternative zum Auto fahren galt, da waren Schutzhütten wie Gasthöfe unabdingbar. Rast und Ruhe, Genuss für Augen, Gaumen, Magen, Kurzweil im Gespräch. Waldcafé, Grotto, Rifugio, alles verheißungsvolle Namen für kleine Gebäude mit großer Attraktivität. Natürlich auch für Autofahrer, doch, man gibt es gerne zu, mit minderem Genuss. Die Erfahrung von Raum und Zeit ist grundsätzlich verschieden. Das unbewusste Gefühl, einen geschützten Ort zu erreichen, auch wenn die Zeit der Wegelagerer passé ist, stellt sich nicht ein, wenn man schon sicher verpackt in einer mobilen Hütte anreist.
Fühlen wir uns längere Zeit wohl in einer leeren Landschaft, ganz ohne Architektur?

Vielleicht erst, wenn wir das mitgeschleppte Zelt aufgebaut haben. Camping, sei es im Biwak oder im Wohnmobil, ist ja eng verwandt mit der Suche nach Unterschlupf in einer Höhle oder unter dem Blätterdach eng stehender Bäume. Das mag der Grund sein, warum Park und Landschaft durch Architektur erst akzeptabel werden, ja schön, wie die Geschichte der Gartenkunst lehrt. Monopteros, Tempel der Diana, Höhle des Eremiten, Chinesischer Turm und künstliche Ruine, Folie und Belvedere: Alles Bauten, die den Ort erhöhen, ihn ins Bewusstsein rücken, die eventuell heute immer noch Sinn haben, sogar wenn es dort keine Bratwurst zu kaufen gibt.
In der Stadt nimmt man zunächst die großen Häuser wahr, aber dann bei genauerem Hinsehen, auch die kleinen Architekturen. Sie sind es oft, die den Charme oder Charakter einer Straße oder eines Platzes ausmachen. Sie gehören zum Alltag der Stadt, somit uns. Eine Trinkhalle, ein Zeitungskiosk, ein Teepavillon, ja sogar Pissoirs, dazu Transformatorenhäuschen, Telefonzellen, abgemagert zu Säulen und Hauben, Bushaltestellen, Blumenstände, Maronibuden – eine Vielfalt, die ein urbanes Raster bildet, darin nicht unähnlich Tschumis Folies in La Villette, wenngleich im lockeren Verbund. Diese kleinen Bauten sind es, ob mobil wie ein Gemüsestand oder fest wie eine Litfaßsäule, die Freiräume besiedeln und im Idealfall veredeln. Sie sind Kristallisationspunkte des sozialen Lebens.

Robert Schäfer

Verrückte Fußnoten der Architektur

Crazy footnotes in architecture

Zu den exotischsten unter den eigenständigen Bautypen, welche die europäische Gartenkunst im Lauf ihrer Geschichte hervorgebracht hat, zählen teils temporäre, teils dauerhafte architektonische Gebilde meist geringer Größe, welche *Follies* (englisch) oder *Folies* (französisch) genannt werden. Wörtlich aus dem Englischen übersetzt bedeutet *Folly* eine Verrücktheit; auf die Architektur übertragen also ein schwer einzuordnendes Bauwerk ohne unmittelbaren Nutzwert. Die französische Ableitung von Folie verweist hingegen auf sehr viel ältere Wurzeln, nämlich auf das lateinische Wort *folia* (französisch *feuille*). Als Folie bezeichnete man denn auch bereits im Mittelalter jede »maison de campagne«, welche vollständig von Grün umgeben war. In der ersten Hälfte des 18. Jahrhunderts entstanden dann in den Grüngürteln rund um die großen Städte Frankreichs Kleinbauten in großer Zahl, ebenfalls Folies genannt, die ausschließlich der privaten Zerstreuung und intimen Vergnügungen dienten. Von hier aus trat diese Gattung von Folies schließlich ihren Siegeszug durch die großen Landschaftsgärten an. Das Prädikat »folle«, entnommen den »folles dépenses«, den riesigen finanziellen Ausgaben also, die für derartig alltagsferne und weitgehend »nutzlose« Bauten aufzubringen waren, verband sich im Volksmund von nun an unauflösbar mit dem Bautyp der Folie. Es verstand sich nämlich beinahe von selbst, dass sich nur ausgesprochen wohlhabende Zeitgenossen derartige architektonische Verschwendungen leisten konnten und wollten.

Auf welchem Terrain aber waren architektonische Kleinkunstwerke dieses Genres ursprünglich angesiedelt, welchen Zweck verfolgten sie ihrer programmatischen Zwecklosigkeit zum Trotz? Zweifellos ist der Garten von Bomarzo nicht die erste, aber vielleicht bekannteste neuzeitliche Schöpfung, die spektakuläre Folies ganz gezielt einsetzt, um dem Protest eines aufgeklärten Renaissancefürsten gegen die restaurierte Bigotterie der römischen Kurie sowie dem privaten Schmerz des alternden Fürsten über das Schwinden seiner Manneskraft bildhaft Ausdruck zu verleihen. Denn der Garten des Fürsten Orsini diente erwiesenermaßen nicht nur, aber auch, dem Zweck, eigens aus Rom eingeladene Kleriker und andere Würdenträger durch komprimierte Denkräume voller heidnischer Bilder und erotischer Anspielungen zutiefst zu verstören.

Folies im Wandel der Zeit: nutzlose Bauten oder subversive Denkmodelle für elysische, arkadische und andere Landschaften.

Follies as the times have changed: useless buildings or subversive monuments for Elysian, Arcadian and other landscapes.

The partly temporary, partly permanent architectonic structures, mostly of smaller size, called follies (or in French: *folies*), count amongst the most exotic of the self-reliant types of buildings which European landscaping has produced in the course of its history. Literally, the English term folly means a foolish act/behaviour/idea; if applied to architecture, it is therefore a type of building without any specific beneficial value, that is difficult to classify. The French derivation folie on the other hand, has much older roots, that is, the Latin word *folia* (French: *feuille*). As far back as the Middle Ages, any "maison de campagne", completely surrounded by green, was also regarded as a folie. In the first half of the 18th century, small buildings similarly called follies then appeared in large numbers, in the green belts surrounding the cities in France, that exclusively served private diversion and intimate amusement. From here, this species of follies finally began its triumphal march through the expansive landscape gardens. The attribute "folle", taken from "folles dépenses" – the enormous financial sums that were collected for largely "useless" buildings of this kind, far remote from everyday life – gained the indelible connotation of a folly in the vernacular for architecture from then on. It was virtually self-explanatory that only particularly wealthy people were able and wanted to afford such architectonic extravagance.

But in what sort of territory did small architectonic masterpieces of this genre originally settle on? What was their purpose despite their programmatic senselessness? The Garden of Bomarzo, without any doubt, is certainly not the first but perhaps the most famous creation of modern times that intentionally implemented the spec-

Anfang des 20. Jahrhunderts gerieten mehr oder weniger nutzlose Bauten in Parks und Landschaft in Verruf. Spätestens Bernard Tschumi rehabilitierte jedoch den Bautyp Folie. Insgesamt 25 dieser roten Bauwerke bilden das berühmte Raster im Parc de la Villette.

More or less useless buildings in the landscape and in parks fell into disrepute at the beginning of the 20th century. With Bernard Tschumi at the latest, the construction type folly was rehabilitated again. All in all 25 of these red structures form the famous grid in the Parc de la Villette.

Das barocke Zeitalter stößt wenig später derartigen Denkräumen weitere Türen auf. Denn es zwingt nicht nur illusionistische Szenarien in seine Interieurs, die mitunter sogar wie begehbare Schädel wirken. Nein, das Barock ist auch imstande, Garten- und Platzräume inhaltlich einander anzugleichen. Plätze reflektieren symbolische Natureruptionen, während Gärten und Parks sich städtebaulicher und architektonischer Mittel bedienen, um Imagination zu inszenieren. So versah André Le Nôtre die Bosketten seiner Parkkonzeption für Versailles mit Namen wie »Salle de Bal« oder »Salle des Festins«, also binnenräumlichen Zuschreibungen, um die Lektüre dieser Freiräume zu erleichtern. Was den Stellenwert der Kunst in diesem Zusammenhang anbelangt, so erscheint Hirschfelds eher beiläufige Anmerkung, »auch die Bildhauerkunst hat nicht unterlassen, an der Verzierung der Gärten, wie der Architectur, Antheil zu nehmen«, äußerst aufschlussreich. Die Ratio ist in diesen Zeiten zwar noch vorhanden, beginnt aber schon, der spekulativen Imagination zu weichen. Gärten und Plätze werden durch den Einsatz von Folies narrativ, episodenhaft, scheinen ferne Ereignisse antizipieren zu wollen; fangen an, sich über Zeit und Raum hinwegsetzend, historisch längst Gewesenes neu zu vergegenwärtigen; beginnen sogar, das eigentlich Nicht-Darstellbare (wie etwa das »Ende der Welt« in Schwetzingen) darzustellen. Dass dies mitunter so angestrengt und komprimiert geschieht, dass das Resultat geradezu ins Lächerliche abgleitet, dokumentieren nicht nur die theatralischen Provinzgärten von Hohenheim und Steinfurt.

Aber erst die Zeit zwischen 1750 und 1850 beschert Europa private Parks, halböffentliche Bildungsgärten, erste öffentliche Volksgärten und zahllose neue Platzanlagen, aus denen Folies nun wirklich nicht mehr wegzudenken sind. Vor allem der englische Landschaftsgarten wird in dieser Zeit zu einer spezifischen Welt des Sublimen, transformiert er doch philosophisch-literarisch-musikalische Bezüge in gepflanzte Landschaftsbilder.

tacular follies to impart a pictorial expression of an enlightened Renaissance prince's protest against the restored bigotry of the Roman Curia and of the ageing prince's personal pain caused by his dwindling virility. For the garden of Prince Orsini, as has been proved, served not only, but also the purpose of utterly bewildering the clergy and other dignitaries invited expressly from Rome, with a concentration of "rooms for reflection", filled with heathen pictures and erotic insinuations.

A short time later, the Baroque Age throws further doors open to rooms for reflection of this nature, as it forces not only illusionist scenarios into its interiors that sometimes even look like skulls one can walk through. No, Baroque is also capable of harmonising the content of green spaces and open spaces. Open spaces reflect symbolic eruptions of nature whereas gardens and parks utilise urban construction and architectonic means to stage the imagination. In this way, André Le Nôtre gave the boscages of his park conception for Versailles names such as "Salle de Bal" or "Salle des Festins", i.e. names for designated interiors in order to facilitate the interpretation of these open spaces. As regards the level of importance of art in this connection, Hirschfeld's rather casual remark, "in the same way as architecture, the art of sculpture could not resist taking part in ornamenting the gardens, either", appears extremely illuminating. Logic is still prevalent during these times, yet is already beginning to give way to speculative imagination. By adding follies, gardens and open spaces become narrative, episodic and seem to want to anticipate far-off events; they begin to serve as a reminder – beyond the limits of time and space – of what has long

Der Garten von Bomarzo gilt als wichtiges Beispiel einer manieristischen Verbindung von Natur und Bildhauerkunst. Der aufgeklärte Renaissancefürst Orsini setzte Pavillons und Folies gezielt ein als Protest gegen die bigotte römische Kurie. Das »Schiefe Haus« wurde zwischen 1564 und 1570 erbaut.

The Garden of Bomarzo is the most important example of a connection between nature and sculpture in a mannerist way. The enlightened Renaissance prince Orsini intentionally implemented pavilions as a protest against the restored bigotry of the Roman Curia. The "Leaning House" was built between 1564 and 1570.

since passed in history; they even begin to present the non-presentable (for instance, the "End of the World" in Schwetzingen). The fact that this sometimes takes place with such effort and concentration and renders the result ridiculous, is documented not only by the theatrical provincial gardens of Hohenheim and Steinfurt.

However, it is not until the period between 1750 and 1850 that Europe has private parks, semi-public educational gardens, the first gardens opened to the public and numerous new open spaces where the presence of follies has now really become a foregone conclusion. The English landscape architecture, above all, becomes a specific world of the sublime during this period, as it indeed transforms philosophical-literary-musical features into pictures set in the landscape. The fact that many gardeners at that time first studied painting and sculpture before they devoted themselves to landscape architecture is not purely accidental. The masterpieces of prominent contemporaries often act as given examples of landscape architecture for educated clients. In addition, English landscape gardens become open green spaces of a philosophical-literary nature. Pückler-Muskau, von Sckell, Lenné and others convert formerly insignificant stretches of land that afterwards arouse the impression of carefully staged condensate of cosmopolitan worldliness. And the follies? Holy groves, dusky grottoes, Egyptian tombs, graves and sphinxes,

Nicht von ungefähr haben viele der Gärtner seinerzeit zunächst eine Ausbildung als Maler oder Bildhauer absolviert, ehe sie sich der Landschaftsgestaltung verschrieben. Kunstwerke prominenter Zeitgenossen fungieren häufig als konkrete Garten-Vorlagen für gebildete Auftraggeber. Darüber hinaus werden englische Gärten zu grünen Lehrräumen philosophisch-literarischer Natur. Pückler-Muskau, von Sckell, Lenné und andere wandeln ehedem unbedeutende Landstriche um, die hernach wie sorgfältig inszenierte Kondensate kosmopolitischer Weltläufigkeit anmuten.

Und die Folies? Heilige Haine, dämmrige Grotten, ägyptische Grabbauten und Sphingen, römische Wasserleitungen, Landhäuser und Kastelle, griechische Tempel und Orakelstätten, romanisch-gotische Traumhäuser, Indianerzelte, Pagoden, Moscheen, Meiereien für Schäferspiele, Gebäude und Räume wie aus gewebten Stoffen, künstliche Ruinen, Urhütten jedweder Provenienz, simulierte archäologische Fundstücke und Brücken aller Zeiten über alle Zeiten hinweg verdichten sich hier zu Freiraum- und Architektur-Collagen, die mitunter authentischer wirken als die Vorbilder, Auftraggebern wie Besuchern mithin das beschwerliche Reisen ersparen. Man bleibt daheim und genießt die elysischen Felder, den ganzen Kosmos erschöpfend zusammengefasst in subversiven architektonischen Gedanken-Passepartouts. Provinzorte wie Schwetzingen, Dessau, Wörlitz oder Muskau werden – wenn auch nur vorübergehend – zum vermeintlichen Nabel der Welt; einer Welt, in der immer waghalsigere Folies Zeit und Raum überspringen, sich Werden und Vergehen, Gewachsenes, Ruinöses und Neuaufgehendes scheinbar mühelos zu eindrucksvollen Symbiosen verbinden. Entlarvend wirkt aus heutiger Perspektive allenfalls, dass listige Bühnenbildner sukzessive zu den gefragtesten Gestaltern derartig ambivalenter arkadischer Landschaften werden.

Eine gänzlich neue Instrumentalisierung erfahren Folies nach den Revolutionen des Jahres 1918. Sie, die als Inkarnation kapitalistischer Verschwendungssucht und Dekadenz galten, verlassen nun ihr als antiquiert und sozial kontraproduktiv deklariertes Terrain gründerzeitlicher Gärten und wandern stattdessen in die schmutzigen Räume und Plätze von Städten, wo sie sich nolens volens in temporäre Agitprop-

Installationen, also politische Ausdrucksträger, verwandeln. In Ermangelung lieferbarer Baumaterialien, konkreter Aufträge und verfügbarer Finanzmittel dienen ephemere Installationen – wie etwa an den zahllosen »Street-Art-Follies« der Russischen Revolutionsarchitektur unschwer abzulesen – zur Projektion schöner neuer Welten kollektiven Zusammenlebens, welche sie möglichst plakativ und aggressiv, vor allem aber politisch korrekt in Szene zu setzen haben. Selbst nicht ausgeführte, also Papier gebliebene Folies haben dem gleichen Zweck zu dienen. Da sie hierbei nicht mehr auf die Bildungshorizonte von Adel und Großbürgertum zurückgreifen können, bedienen sie sich zunehmend holzschnittartig vergröberter, häufig sogar ausgesprochen populistischer Ausdrucksweisen.

Doch scheint die Politisierung der Folies ihren Untergang nur noch beschleunigt zu haben. Denn die in der zweiten Hälfte der zwanziger Jahre auch international erfolgreiche Neue Sachlichkeit schwört allen gefühlsbetonten architektonischen Entäußerungen ab. Stattdessen sind jetzt Zweckhaftigkeit, Rationalität und konstruktive Beständigkeit gefragt. Selbst tem-

Die russischen Revolutionäre sahen in Folies und Lusthäuschen Ausdruck kapitalistischer Dekadenz. Temporäre Bauten sollten revolutionäre Ideale transportieren. Viele, auch größere Bauten gingen übers Entwurfsstadium nicht hinaus. Wladimir Tatlin schlug ein Denkmal für die III. Internationale in Petrograd (Sankt Petersburg) vor.

Russian revolutionaries saw follies and summerhouses as an expression of capitalistic decadence. Temporary buildings were to transport revolutionary ideals. Many structures, small and large, were not realized but remained a draft only. Wladimir Tatlin suggested a monument for the Third International in Petrograd (Saint Petersburg).

Roman water-pipes, villas and citadels, Greek temples, Romanesque-Gothic dream-houses, Indian tents, pagodas, mosques, farms for pastoral play, buildings and rooms as if of woven materials, artificial ruins, primeval huts of whatever origin, simulated archaeological findings and bridges of all epochs are concentrated here to collages of open space and architecture, that sometimes look more authentic than the originals and thus save the clients and visitors the inconvenience of travelling. One stays at home and enjoys the Elysian fields, the entire cosmos, exhaustively concentrated in subversive architectonic passe-partouts of thought. Provincial sites such as Schwetzingen, Dessau, Wörlitz or Muskau become – even if only temporarily – the imaginary navel of the world; a world in which more and more daring follies surpass the limits of time and space, are born and pass away, where the grown, the ruinous and the newly dawning join together with apparent ease to form impressive symbioses. At all events, from today's perspective, it appears unmasking that cunning scenic designers are successively becoming the most demanded designers of such ambivalent Arcadian landscapes.

Follies experienced an entirely new instrumentalisation after the revolutions of 1918. Once deemed as an incarnation of the capitalistic addiction to extravagance and decadence, they leave their now proclaimed antiquated and socially contra-productive terrain in the late 19th century gardens, and instead, wander into the dirty urban rooms and open spaces, where they change, nolens volens, into temporary agitprop installations, i.e. political expressionists. Lacking supplies of building materials, firm orders and available means of finance, ephemeral installations serve –

as is not difficult to discern, for instance, in the countless "Street Art Follies" of Russian Revolution architecture – for projecting beautiful new worlds of collective communes that they have to stage in the best displayed and most aggressive way possible, but above all politically correct. Even follies not yet carried out, i.e. still on paper, have the same purpose to serve. As they are no longer able to fall back here on the educational horizons of aristocracy and the upper class, they increasingly use coarsely chiseled and frequently even extremely populist forms of expression.

In fact, the politicization of the follies seems to have only accelerated their ruin. For the so-called New Practicality, which was also successful internationally in the second half of the 20's, renounces all emotional architectonic expression.

porären Gebäuden und Installationen begegnet man inzwischen mit einem ebenso unerbittlichen wie humorlosen Zweck- und Reinheitsempfinden. So wäre damals wohl niemand ernsthaft auf die Idee gekommen, Le Corbusiers Pavillon de L'Esprit Nouveau von 1925 oder Mies van der Rohes Barcelona-Pavillon von 1929 als Folies zu bezeichnen, obwohl es sich zweifelsfrei um solche handelte. Diese bewusste Verdrängung und Tabuisierung all dessen, was auf- und anreizende, raum-zeit-überspringende dreidimensionale Bilder von beschränkter Haltbarkeit tangiert, sollte sich bis weit in die sechziger und siebziger Jahre des 20. Jahrhunderts hinein halten.

Erst seit dieser Zeit sind wieder frische, unverbrauchte Aktivitäten zur Rückgewinnung von Denkräumen zu beobachten: Aktivitäten, die freilich fast allesamt im Grenzbereich zwischen Kunstinstallation, Spurensuche, Landschaftsgestaltung und Architektur angesiedelt sind. Das macht es nun noch schwerer als es bislang schon war, Typen und Topoi verschwundener, aktueller und künftiger Folies präziser einzugrenzen. Denn da gibt es eine heterogene Fülle vorzüglicher älterer Beispiele, wie die der Land Art, die frühen Projekte von Hollein und Pichler, Superstudio, Haus-Rucker-Co,

Hans Dieter Schaal, Dan Graham, Hansjörg Voth, Ian Hamilton Finlay oder jüngere und jüngste Folies von Bernard Tschumi, Zaha Hadid, Coop Himmelb(l)au, van Lieshout, Adriaan Geuze und vielen anderen mehr. Was die dazugehörigen Installationen jedoch trotz aller Heterogenität vereint, ist das Bemühen um die Schaffung wirklich neuer Denkräume oder Denkorte. Derartige Arbeiten zwingen nämlich den jeweiligen Betrachter, wieder über einen spezifischen Ort, eine spezifische Region nachzudenken; wobei das geforderte Maß des Nachdenkens alle Konventionen sprengt: gewesene Ereignisse, literarische Fußnoten zu diesem oder einem wesensverwandten Ort, Juxtapositionen historischer Entwicklungen, fiktive Archäologien, Fragen nach dem, was hier alles hätte stattfinden können oder vielleicht einmal stattfinden wird, und immer wieder Brechungen der Realität zugunsten ge- oder verworfener gestalterischer Kommentare. Beiläufig gesagt, passen letztere nur selten in das Schema postmoderner Behüb-

Instead, practicability, rationality and constructive durability are called for. Even temporary buildings and installations rouse the feeling for purpose and cleanliness, that is similarly devoid of any pity and humour. Earlier nobody would have ever seriously dreamed of calling Le Corbusier's Pavillon de L'Esprit Nouveau of 1925 or Mies van der Rohe's Barcelona Pavillon of 1929 follies, although there is no doubt that they were. This conscious suppression, or taboo-culture regarding anything that resembles provocation, incitement, three-dimensional pictures of restricted durability exceeding the limits of space and time, was to endure as long as the 1960's or 1970's.

Fresh, unexhausted activity for winning back rooms of thought, was not observed again until after this time, i.e. activity – which certainly is almost all to be found along the borders linking art installation, track-hunting, landscape architecture and architecture. This of course makes it even more difficult than ever before to define the types and topoi of passed, current and future follies more precisely. For there is a heterogeneous wealth of excellent older examples, such as those of Land Art, the early projects of Hollein and Pichler, Superstudio, Haus-Rucker-Co, Hans Dieter Schaal, Dan Graham, Hansjörg Voth, Ian Hamilton Finlay or the later and latest follies of Bernard Tschumi, Zaha Hadid, Coop Himmelb(l)au, van Lieshout, Adriaan Geuze and many others. In all these associated examples, however, despite their heterogeneity, there is the common effort to create really new rooms of thought or places of thought. For works of this kind force the observer involved to reflect again on a specific place, a specific region; whereby the required depth of reflection bursts all conven-

Aktionen zwischen Kunst, Architektur und Landschaftsarchitektur in den sechziger und siebziger Jahren regen Betrachter wiederum an, sich mit spezifischen Orten auseinanderzusetzen. Das Bild zeigt die Installation »Schräge Ebene« von Haus-Rucker-Co am Wiener Naschmarkt im Jahr 1976.

Campaigns drawing on art, architecture and landscape architecture in the sixties and seventies stimulate the observers to concern themselves with specific places.
The photograph shows the installation "Sloping Plane" of Haus-Rucker-Co at the Naschmarkt in Vienna from 1976.

tions. Past events, literary footnotes to this place or another related in kind, juxtapositions of historical developments, fictive archaeology, questions about everything that could have happened here or might still happen, and breaks with reality again and again, in favour of spontaneous or base artistic comments. Casually spoken, the latter only seldom fit into the picture of post-modern beautifying strategies, as they are almost always harassing subliminally, challenging, sometimes even causing goose-flesh, but mostly a liberating sigh of relief.

In short, at the latest since Bernard Tschumi's Parisian Parc de la Villette (1983-95) follies are fit for good society again, which of course by no means implies their general acceptance or general understandability. Small, temporary and therefore sometimes all the more spectacular species of "flying buildings" also fit quite well at present in the concept of communes that are seeking models of thought – clamouring for publicity and low-priced because not planned for all eternity – against the devastation and misuse of their public spaces. Thus in 1990, the Dutch town

schungs-Strategien, sind sie doch unterschwellig fast immer bedrängend, herausfordernd, verursachen sie manchmal sogar Gänsehaut, meist aber befreiendes Aufatmen.

Kurzum, spätestens seit Bernard Tschumis Pariser Parc de la Villette (1983 bis 1995) sind Folies wieder salonfähig, was freilich keinesfalls ihre generelle Anerkennung oder allgemeine Verständlichkeit bedeutet. Kleine, temporäre und deshalb mitunter um so spektakulärere Spezies der Gattung »fliegende Bauten« passen derzeit auch ganz gut in das Konzept solcher Kommunen, welche nach publicityträchtigen, preisgünstigen, weil nicht für alle Ewigkeit gedachten Denkmodellen gegen Verödung und Missbrauch ihrer öffentlichen Räume suchen.

So hat die niederländische Stadt Groningen im Jahre 1990 Rem Koolhaas, Bernard Tschumi, Coop Himmelb(l)au und andere internationale Architekturgrößen damit beauftragt, eine ganze Serie unterschiedlicher Folies im Weichbild der Stadt zu installieren. Die Aktion war so erfolgreich, dass die japanische Stadt Osaka wenig später sogar mit einem internationalen Symposium zum Thema Folies nebst entsprechenden Demonstrationsobjekten im Maßstab 1:1 mitzog. Bei derartigen Aktionen werden freilich die Grenzen zwischen großer dauerhafter Architektur und kleiner künstlerischer Ad-hoc-Installation immer fließender und diffuser. Wenn etwa Takesaki Masaharus »Kihoku Astronomical Museum« für die japanische Stadt Ichinari (1995), obgleich aus Beton gefügt, schon per se wie ein gigantisches Gestell heterogener, scheinbar provisorisch miteinander verflochtener Körper im Raum wirkt, dann beginnt man an der bewährten Unterscheidung zwischen festem Zweckbau und flüchtigem didaktischen Denkmodell zu zweifeln. Und wenn Antoine Predocks »American Heritage Center« in Laramie,USA, aus dem Jahr 1993 eher einem soeben gelandeten und gleich wieder abhebenden Ufo gleicht als einem konventionellen Museum, dann präsentiert es sich ganz bewusst als Camouflage einer flüchtigen Folie und nicht als würdevoller Bau, auf ewig fest verankert in der Erde.

Das Thema Folie sorgt also wieder für Diskussionen. Vielleicht werden provokante Verrücktheiten temporärer Gegenwelten, zumindest die besten unter ihnen, dereinst einmal weit höher bewertet werden als die willfährige Affirmation und verzweifelte Redundanz unserer ordinären Alltagsarchitektur. Folies als stadtlandschaftliche Überlebensstrategie, wäre das nicht ein wenig zu schön um wahr zu sein?

Groningen commissioned Rem Koolhaas, Bernard Tschumi, Coop Himmelb(l)au and other big names in international architecture with the installation of a whole series of the most differing follies in the outskirts of the town. This campaign was so successful that the Japanese town Osaka even joined in a short time later with an international symposium on the topic of follies together with relevant objects for demonstration in the scale of 1:1. In campaigns of this kind the boundaries linking large-scale architecture of a permanent kind with small artistic ad hoc installations of course tend to dwindle and become more diffuse. If, for instance, Takesaki Masaharu's "Kihoku Astronomical Museum" for the Japanese town Ichinari (1995), although joined together by concrete, looks even per se like a gigantic framework of heterogeneous bodies in space that have seemingly been woven together temporarily, then one begins to doubt the accepted differentiation between a building serving a specific purpose and a short-lived, didactic model of thought. And if Antoine Predock's "American Heritage Center" in Laramie/USA (1993) more resembles an UFO that has just landed and is taking off again, than a conventional museum, then it is presenting itself quite intentionally as a camouflage of a short-lived folly and not as a dignified building. The folly topic is therefore giving rise to discussion once again. Perhaps provocative crazes of temporary, opposite worlds – at least the best amongst them – will be assessed far higher in days to come than the compliant affirmation and desperate redundancy of our ordinary everyday architecture. Follies – an urban landscape strategy for survival – would this not be somewhat too good to be true?

Kleine Strukturen – Objekte im öffentlichen Raum

Small structures in public open space

Approach. Every time a new assignment begins, every time a factor is considered or a line consciously or unconsciously drawn, the search for a metaphor begins, for a phrase that says everything in a few words yet leaves enough scope for all kinds of the interpretation that becomes necessary in the creative process.

This involves questions posed from various points of view or arising from changes in opinion. How should shape be determined – by the underlying structure or skin that covers it? What happens if you stack something up, suspend it or layer it? In what way do form and function change at night, with the passing of the day, and when seen from new positions?

Ansatz. Mit jeder neuen Aufgabe, jeder Überlegung, jedem bewusst – oder unbewusst – gesetzten Strich, beginnt die Suche nach einer Metapher, nach einem Satz, der mit wenigen Worten alles zusammenfasst und doch genug Spielraum lässt für jegliche Interpretation, die im Prozess des Machens nötig wird. Fragen, gestellt aus unterschiedlichen Positionen, veränderter Ansicht. Was gibt die Form vor – die Hülle oder der Körper darunter? Was passiert, wenn Gleiches gestapelt, gehängt oder geschichtet wird? Wie verändert sich die Funktion und die Gestalt, bei Tag und bei Nacht, zu unterschiedlichen Zeitpunkten und von verschiedenen Positionen aus betrachtet ?

Denksatz. Der Bruch im Denken ist die Bedingung, um Konvention und Tradition neu zu interpretieren und zu variieren. Zuvor muss rückwärts gegangen werden, analysiert und der Ursa-

Regina Schineis

Kleine Bauten stehen wie Kunstobjekte im Augsburger Stadtraum und erfüllen doch eine klare, technische Funktion.

Embodying an unusual design in each case, the small-sized structures fulfil a technical function yet resemble art objects at the same time.

Das Einstiegsbauwerk auf dem Augsburger Königsplatz verwirrt die Passanten: Handelt es sich um eine technische Konstruktion oder um ein Kunstwerk? Tags schimmert das Grün der Bäume durch das Gewebe seiner Hülle, bei Dunkelheit bringen zwischen dem Netz angebrachte Strahler die Konstruktion zum Leuchten und verwandeln sie in eine Lichtskulptur.

Passers-by are never quite sure whether the entrance structure at the Königsplatz area in Augsburg is part of a technical utility or whether it is an art object. During the day, the green of the trees shimmers through its outer mesh; at night, lights inserted between the underlying ribbing make the entrance building shine as if it were a light sculpture.

Eine vorgefertigte Box aus Stahlbeton beherbergt die Trafostation. Mit einem orangen Anstrich versehen, wird sie zusätzlich von einem Drahtgewebe umhüllt. Vom Dach herabrieselndes Wasser gefriert im Winter und bildet eine weitere umhüllende Schicht.

The transformer station is housed in a prefabricated shell of reinforced concrete covered by an outer skin of wire mesh. In winter, water trickling down from the roof tends to freeze, covering the mesh over the orange-painted walls with a second skin.

Philosophy. Disrupting the way we think is a prerequisite to coming up with new interpretations or variations of conventional and traditional viewpoints. Beforehand it is necessary to step back, analyse and get down to the roots of the matter, and from there retrace one's steps along the expected path but in an oblique manner. This is to enable an upsetting of orderly layers of thought in order to integrate the potential for future developments. To see the city as a whole, made up of mosaic pieces, alive in every state and condition.

Intention. In expressing the results of creative approaches in tangible form, it is important to adhere to the leitmotif of the concept down to the very last detail despite all constraints, animosities or tendencies to get carried away. The goal is to achieve clarity and simplicity of expression and in this way return architecture to our busy everyday lives. This involves narrowing down the choice of possible materials to a very few and using them in an effortless way where they are least expected, supported by the shaping qualities of light as a delineating medium.

Entrance structure. In a public park, a rarely-used downward passage that doubles as an outlet for the waste air produced by subterranean transformers is the only indication that the park has an underground dimension. What was required here was a protective shelter for the simple function of downward movement, for the stairway. Something transparent in effect but clearly limiting access. The stainless steel mesh that loosely covers the underlying stainless steel ribbing necessitated – due to its properties – a large number of supports that give the substructure its ribbing effect. At night, the cover is opaque when seen from certain angles but transparent from others. The structure begins to shine, becomes a light object in the night-time park.

Transformer station. An outer layer was applied on-site to a prefabricated shell of reinforced concrete. The material chosen was the herringbone wire mesh used for technical purposes in streetcar operation. The underlying framework was fitted with the mesh and attached to the coloured walls of the transformation station, which provides trams with electricity. Water spouts break through the irregular composition of the metal frames and freezes in winter, covering the mesh with a second skin. Light shining up from around the ground level makes the red

che auf den Grund gegangen werden, um von dort aus in nicht geradliniger Weise den erwarteten Weg noch einmal zurückzulegen. Dadurch soll den geordneten Schichten die Störung ermöglicht werden, um Potenziale für zukünftige Entwicklungen zu integrieren, Stadt als Ganzes zu sehen, zusammengesetzt aus Mosaiksteinen, und in jedem Zustand lebendig.

Vorsatz. Bei der Umsetzung der kreativen Ansätze in erlebbaren Raum ist es dann wesentlich, den roten Faden des Konzeptes gegen alle Ausuferungen, Anfeindungen und Zwänge bis ins Detail beizubehalten. Ziel ist es, zu Klarheit und Einfachheit in der Ausdruckskraft des gebauten Raumes zu gelangen und dadurch die Architektur zurückzuholen in unseren bewegten Alltag. Und das durch die Reduzierung auf nur wenige Materialien, die an ungewohnter Stelle spielerisch eingesetzt werden, unterstützt von Licht, das als raumbegrenzendes Medium gestaltgebend wirkt.

Einstiegsbauwerk. Ein selten genutzter Abgang im öffentlichen Park, der zugleich die Abluft der unterirdischen Transformatoren abfließen lassen muss. Einziges Zeichen für Unterirdisches im Grün des öffentlichen Raumes. Zugleich Hülle und Schutz für eine einfache Funktion – die vertikale Bewegung, den Treppenlauf. Transparent in seiner Gestalt und doch den Zutritt begrenzend. Das Edelstahlgewebe, eine lose Haut über das Gerippe aus Edelstahlrahmen gelegt, verlangt aufgrund seiner Materialeigenschaft nach der Vielzahl der Rahmen, was wiederum die Konstruktion zum

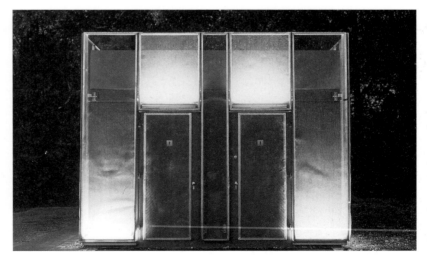

Halbrahmen aus Flachstahl bilden die Konstruktion für die Fahrgastunterstände. Zwischen den Rahmen sind unterschiedliche Elemente wie Infowände, Werbevitrinen oder Sitzbänke eingebaut. Die farbigen Glaselemente zeigen die Distanz zum Stadtzentrum an: Im Zentrum leuchten sie in hellem Orange, am Stadtrand in dunklem Rot.

Flat steel half-frames, the basic elements of the transit shelters, provide space for illuminated information panels, seats, advertising showcases, rubbish bins and loudspeakers. The rear glass panels are coloured to indicate the distance away from the downtown area, starting out with pale orange at the city centre and progressing to scarlet on the outskirts.

Entrance structure, transformer station, transit shelter and mobile base station
Client: Stadtwerke Augsburg – Verkehrs GmbH
Architecture: Büro für Architektur und Städtebau, Regina Schineis, Augsburg
Planning and construction: Entrance structure: 1999 – 2000;
transformer station, transit shelter and mobile base station: 2000 – 2001

The small structures have won various design awards (Renault Award for Traffic Design: entrance structure in 2000, mobile base station in 2001, special mention: transit shelters in 2003; Public Design Award, special mention: transit shelters in 2003).

Im quadratischen Raum der Funkfeststation befinden sich Schaltschränke zum Betrieb der Straßenbahnlinie. Der doppelt verglaste Kubus ist mit einem acht Zentimeter breiten Kupferband umwickelt. Es steht für die Kupfertransformatoren, die im Inneren die Funkverbindung herstellen und schützt gleichzeitig die Glasbox. Tagsüber leuchtet das Kupfer in der Sonne, nachts schimmert das Grün des hinterleuchteten Glaskubus hindurch.

The interior of the mobile base station contains the control cabinets involved in transmitting the radio signals required for operation of a tram line. The double-glazed structure is wrapped in copper bands. These stand for the copper transformers that create the radio contacts, and help protect the glass casing from damage. At night the green light inside the glass cube shines between the bands, which glow orange in the sun during the day.

Gerippe macht. In der Nacht verändert sich die Transparenz, wechselnde Positionen zeigen veränderte Durchsicht. Das Bauwerk beginnt zu leuchten, wird zum Lichtobjekt im nächtlichen Park.

Trafostation. Die vorgefertigte Box aus Stahlbeton bekommt vor Ort ihre Haut. Gewählt wird ein pfeilgewelltes Drahtgestricke, üblicherweise eingesetzt als Schnittschutzmatte für die Wandungen einer Straßenbahn. Die Rahmen, gefüllt mit dem Gestricke, werden vor die mit einem farbigen Anstrich versehene Trafostation, die für den Betriebsstrom der Straßenbahn sorgt, gehängt. Wasserspeier durchbrechen die Kompositionen der unterschiedlichen Formate der Metallrahmen, das Wasser gefriert im Winter und zieht eine zweite Haut über das Gestricke. Ein am Boden umlaufendes Lichtband bringt nachts das Rot zum Leuchten und das Gestricke zum Flimmern, die gebaute Grenzen lösen sich auf.

Fahrgastunterstände. Die schutzgebende Funktion der Konstruktion wird reduziert auf einfache Elemente. Halbrahmen aus zusammengesetzten Flachstählen werden aneinandergereiht. Zwischen die Rahmen werden die notwendigen dienenden Objekte für den Fahrgast eingebaut: leuchtende Infoelemente, Sitzbänke, Werbevitrinen, Mülleimer, Lautsprecher. Die Rückwand wird verglast, transparentes Siebdruckglas setzt Akzente, nimmt den Farbton der Umgebung auf, verstärkt ihn, und verschafft den funktionalen Fahrgastunterständen Präsenz im städtischen Raum. Gleichzeitig wird durch die Steigerung der Anzahl und der Intensität der Farben Distanz ablesbar gemacht. Je mehr Farbe sichtbar wird, desto weiter bewegt man sich aus der Stadt, von hellem Orange zu dunklem Rot. Die Bewegung durch die Stadt wird durch die Fahrgastunterstände räumlich erfahrbar.

Funkfeststation. Das unregelmäßig gewickelte Band verpackt eine Glasbox und steht als Metapher für die Kupfertransformatoren, die in den Schaltschränken die Funkverbindung herstellen. Gleichzeitig wirkt das Band als Schutz vor Überhitzung des Inneren und vor Beschädigung der tragenden Glashülle. Es entsteht tagsüber ein Spiel mit Licht und Schatten, je nach Position und Sonneneinstrahlung verändert sich die Ansicht. Die Kupferbänder glänzen in der Sonne, zeigen ihr Alter durch ihre wechselnde Farbigkeit der Patina. Der warme Lichtton löst die Konturen auf und harmoniert mit dem Grün der Scheiben und dem Kupfer der Wicklung. In der Dämmerung beginnt das Innere zwischen den Bändern durchzuschimmern, das Licht schafft einen Negativabdruck der Wicklung, bringt das Innere nach Außen.

structure shine at night and the mesh shimmer, blurring the edges of the structure.

Transit shelters. The protective function of the structure is fulfilled by means of simple, minimalist elements divided up by flat steel half-frames lined up in a row. Objects serving passenger needs – illuminated information panels, seats, advertising showcases, rubbish bins and loudspeakers – are fitted into the spaces between the half frames. The rear wall is made of glass. Transparent screen-printed panels introduce accentuation, take up local colour, reflect it and provide the functional structure with a stronger presence in urban settings. At the same time, distance is made apparent by the increase in the number and intensity of the colours. The more colours are featured, the further one is moving away from the city, from pale orange to scarlet. The shelters underscore progress through the city.

Mobile base station. The glass structure is wrapped in copper bands as a metaphor for the copper transformers that create radio contacts in control cabinets. At the same time, the bands help prevent the interior from overheating and protect the glass casing from damage. The result is a play of light and shade, with the station changing in appearance depending on the angle of the sun and the position from which it is seen. The copper bands shine in the sunlight, and will develop a deepening patina that shows their age. The warm lighting makes the contours swim, and harmonises with the green elements and the copper windings. At dusk, the light shines out between the copper bands, creating a negative version of the outer windings, bringing the inside to the outside.

Bild und Raum

Image and space

The Observatorium group of Dutch artists works on interfaces. They build pavilions they call "observatories" that invite you to introspection out in public. Observatories have been set up in New York and in Hoeksche Waard, and most recently one called "Het Otium" arose in a field near Groningen. These small structures are about the potential of architecture, yet without being architecture themselves. Instead of the art of building, it is the art of observation that inspires this group's production. They work with architecture and landscape architecture the way other artists would work with painting or sculpture, calligraphy or the aesthetics of words. Observatorium exemplifies both the architectural and the garden arts in the fine arts. Therein lies the impetus that their works can give to contemporary architecture and landscape architecture.

Unlike what architects and garden architects are usually obliged to do, the group does not represent a regional or even local point of departure in their creative approach. Art being "liberal", it does not have to express the "spirit of place" but is free to create one in the first place. In spite of this independence, the Observatorium group's work and the recognition they now receive is understandable only in the context of the generally modern and cosmopolitan self-image of the Netherlands, where questions of identity and self-awareness became important nevertheless.

The observatories are more than works of art whose mere presence is meant to attract attention to a place and thus increase its value. In fact, the subject of the observatories themselves is the detached gaze of the independent viewer, who no longer looks in order to prepare uses but whose gaze itself creates the increased social value. These small

Die niederländische Künstlergruppe Observatorium arbeitet an Schnittstellen. Pavillons, »Observatorien« genannt, laden in der Öffentlichkeit zur Innerlichkeit ein. Observatorien entstanden in New York ebenso wie in Hoeksche Waard oder zuletzt »Het Otium« auf einem Acker nahe Groningen. Die kleinen Bauwerke thematisieren Möglichkeiten der Architektur, ohne selbst zur Architektur zu werden. Nicht die Baukunst, sondern die Kunst der Beobachtung inspiriert das Werk der Gruppe. Sie arbeiten mit Architektur und Landschaftsarchitektur, wie andere Künstler mit Malerei oder Bildhauerei, mit Kalligraphie oder der Ästhetik der Wörter. Bau- wie Gartenkunst werden durch Observatorium in der bildenden Kunst exemplifiziert. Hier liegt der Impuls, den diese Arbeiten der zeitgenössischen Architektur wie der Landschaftsarchitektur geben können.

Die Gruppe vertritt in ihrer künstlerischen Haltung, anders als es Bau- und Gartenkünstler meist tun müssen, keinen regionalen oder gar lokalen Ansatz. Die »freie« Kunst muss eben nicht den »Geist des Ortes« zum Ausdruck bringen, sondern darf diesen erst schaffen. Verständlich werden das Werk sowie die gegenwärtige Beachtung der Gruppe Observatorium trotz dieser Bindungslosigkeit nur vor dem Hintergrund der sich generell als modern und weltläufig verstehenden Niederlande, wo gleichwohl die Frage nach Identität und Selbst-Bewusstsein wichtig wurde.

Die Observatorien sind mehr als Kunstwerke, deren bloße Anwesenheit der Aufmerksamkeits- und damit der Wertsteigerung eines Raumes dienen soll. Denn die Observatorien selbst thematisieren den distanzierten Blick des freien Betrachters, der nicht mehr blickt, um eine Nutzung vorzubereiten, sondern dessen Schauen selbst einen gesellschaftlichen Mehrwert schafft. Diese Kleinbauten sind also Kunstobjekte der Selbstvergewisserung des Ich im öffentlichen Raum. Indem sie die Distanzierung des Menschen von einem Ort als gesellschaftliche Veränderung zum Thema machen, gelingt es, die veränderte Wahrnehmung, die ästhetische Distanz des Betrachters eines Objektes nicht nur herauszufordern, sondern sie zugleich in Frage zu stellen.

Thies Schröder
Andre Dekker

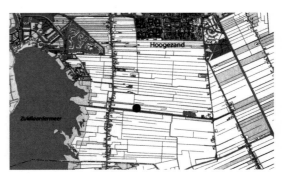

Die Gruppe Observatorium versteht ihre Bauten als Testräume für die Wahrnehmung gesellschaftlicher Veränderung.
The Observatorium artists' group sees their structures as spaces for testing the perception of social change.

Großflächige Landwirtschaft dominiert die »Veenkoloniën« am Zuidlardermeer in der Nähe von Groningen. Die Gruppe Observatorium baute mitten in der Agrarlandschaft »Otium Leinewijk«, eine von mehreren öffentlichen Skulpturen im ehemaligen Moor.

Large-scale farming dominates the landscape in the "Veen Colonies" by the Zuidlardersee near Groningen. In the midst of this agricultural landscape the Observatorium group built "Otium Leinewijk", one of several public sculptures in the former moors.

structures are therefore artworks that confirm the self in public space. By making their subject the social change represented by the detachment of people from a place, they succeed not only in challenging the changed perception and aesthetic distance of the viewer of an object but also in questioning it.

Have the observatories thus integrated and overcome that social function of anchoring that normally belongs to agrarian or Romantic natural landscapes? Do observatories create a sense of "home"? At least they move within this range. Yet they do not suggest tradition or security in the cultivated landscape but the possibility of confronting its transformation with cultural concentration. While in the history of garden architecture small structures such as pavilions or bridges were once pilot projects for architectural innova-

tion, the observatories today are spaces for testing the perception of processes of social change.

Observatorium makes observing something out of everyday curiosity into a creatively staged challenge. "We try to create space for individual experiences in the larger social, economic and ecological context, whether in the density of an urban landscape, in a public park, or in the open countryside. Ultimately we feel it is necessary to design public spaces that link these different and separate worlds and develop parameters for individual experience". This is what the group believes in, as illustrated in the "Otium Leinewijk" project in a former moor region near Groningen.

The moor was cultivated in the 19th century; in the 20th it was repeatedly divided up into lots for large-scale subsidized agriculture. With its

Der Bau dient Radfahrern und Wanderern als Rastplatz und Aussichtspunkt. Die roten Betonquader erinnern an die ursprüngliche Bodenhöhe vor dem Abbau des braunroten Torfs.

The structure serves cyclists and hikers as a place to rest and enjoy the view. The red concrete blocks refer to the original ground level before the brownish red peat was extracted.

Die veränderbaren Module der Skulptur bestehen aus Stahlskeletten und Holzpaletten, die die Linearität der Agrarlandschaft widerspiegeln. Die Künstler verzichteten auf Fenster in den Betonquadern. Stattdessen gewähren in die Wände eingelassene Stahlrohre Blicke auf die Landschaft und den Innenraum.

The variable modules of the sculpture consist of steel skeletons and wooden pallets that reflect the linearity of the agricultural landscape. The artists did not furnish the concrete boxes with windows. Steel pipes set into the walls provide views of the landscape and the interior instead.

Haben die Observatorien damit jene gesellschaftliche Verankerungsfunktion integriert und überwunden, die üblicherweise agrar- oder naturromantischen Sujets zukommt? Schaffen Observatorien »Heimat«? Sie arbeiten zumindest in diesem Spannungsfeld. Doch sie suggerieren nicht Tradition oder Geborgenheit in der Kulturlandschaft, sondern die Möglichkeit, deren Transformation mittels kultureller Konzentration zu begegnen. Waren kleine Bauten wie Pavillons oder Brücken in der Geschichte der Gartenkunst einst Testobjekte für bautechnische Innovationen, so sind die Observatorien heute Testräume für die Wahrnehmung gesellschaftlicher Veränderungsprozesse.

Observatorium macht das Beobachten aus alltäglicher Neugierde zur künstlerisch inszenierten Herausforderung. »Wir versuchen, Raum zu schaffen für individuelle Erfahrungen inmitten von sozialen, ökonomischen oder ökologischen Zusammenhängen, sei es in der Dichte einer Stadtlandschaft, in einem öffentlichen Park oder im offenen ländlichen Raum. Schlussendlich halten wir es für notwendig, öffentliche Räume zu gestalten, die diese unterschiedlichen und getrennten Welten verbinden, und Parameter für eine individuelle Erfahrung zu entwickeln«, lautet das Credo der Gruppe – so auch beim Projekt »Otium Leinewijk« in einem ehemaligen Moorgebiet nahe Groningen.

Das Moorgebiet wurde im 19. Jahrhundert kultiviert, im 20. Jahrhundert mehrfach zur Nutzung durch großflächige, subventionierte Landwirtschaft parzelliert. Die Landschaft mit geraden Wegen und Kanälen wirkt weit, der Horizont fern. Kartoffeln werden im großen Stil angebaut. Der Ort bietet also kaum Naturgenuss und Entspannung – allein schon wegen des ständigen, schneidenden Windes. Die Kommission für Flurbereinigung der Moorkolonien, seit 15 Jahre beschäftigt mit der Neugestaltung des ehemaligen Moorgebietes, beauftragte die Künstler, eine Skulptur zu schaffen, welche die Eigenart der Moorlandschaft sowohl thematisiert als auch erfahrbar macht.

Observatorium wählte einen Standort an einem breiten Kanal, zugänglich nur für Wanderer und Radfahrer. An der Grenze zwischen der lieblichen, alten Landschaft des Zuidlaardermeer und der maschinengerechten Nutzlandschaft bauten die Künstler eine Skulptur als Landmarke und Tor zur Weite des Landes. Die Form dieser Landschaft veränderte sich in den letzten hundert Jahren drei Mal und wird auch in Zukunft noch viele Wandlungen durchmachen. So musste auch diese Skulptur variabel sein. Außerdem sollte auf Wunsch der Künstler die Skulptur für Vorbeikommende als Rastplatz, Aussichtspunkt und Aufenthaltsort dienen.

Otium Leinewijk, Hoogezand-Sappemeer, The Netherlands
Client: Commission on re-allocation of arable land in the moor colonies, Gronin-gen-Drente; curator of the Semlinie art route: Loes Heebink
Design: Observatorium, Rotterdam (Geert van de Camp, Andre Dekker, Ruud Reutelingsperger)
Planning and realisation: 1998 – 2002
Costs: 120,000 Euro

straight paths and canals the landscape appears broad, the horizon distant. Potatoes are farmed in agro-business style. Thus the place does not offer much in the way of pleasure and relaxation in a natural setting – if only because of the constant biting wind. The commission on re-allocation of arable land in the moor colonies, which has been working on reorganizing the former moors for the last 15 years, commissioned the artists to create a sculpture that not only is about the uniqueness of the moor landscape but also allows this uniqueness to be experienced.

Observatorium chose a location next to a wide canal, accessible only to hikers and cyclists. On the borderline between the charming old landscape of the Zuidlaardersee (lake) and the utilitarian landscape of mechanized agriculture, the artists built a sculpture as a landmark and gateway to the expanse of the countryside. The form of this landscape changed three times in the last one hundred years and will undergo many more changes in the future. Hence this sculpture had to be variable also. Besides, the artists wanted the sculpture to serve as a place for passers-by to stop and linger and as a lookout.

The work consists of three steel skeletons with wooden pallets. Inserted in the skeleton of the waterside structure are two lodgings that can be locked up. The walls and roofs are faced with a layer of red cast concrete. Sixteen steel pipes pierce through the concrete walls and provide views of canals, chimneys, farmyards and gas production plants. All parts of the building are standardized like modules. The variability of the observatory refers to the constant change of the landscape. The red lodgings recall the original ground level in this area before the brown-red peat was extracted. The pallets reflect the appearance of the region from a bird's eye perspective: extended fields and ditches broken up by roads and canals.

The artists decided to give the public sculpture to a private individual who uses the "Otium Leinewijk" and looks after the maintenance and administration. The administrator of the sculpture is free to alter or enlarge it. Of course this person is not allowed to deny access to anyone, for this is a public work of art in private custody.

Thus Observatorium stages space in public – a public-space space, as it were. The artists do not design space as static but express the relativity of spaces and objects and of viewers and their field of vision. In each of their observatories the group has the same aim: to make the viewers of a work of art become viewers of themselves. However, the observatories do not cast the viewers back onto themselves, such as in the mirror pavilions by Dan Graham, but embrace them. The fact that the shelter questions rather than expresses the identity of the viewer visiting an observatory creates an irritating element that makes these observatories evoke the opposite of the desire for home and domesticity.

Das Werk besteht aus drei Stahlskeletten mit hölzernen Paletten. In das Skelett des Baus am Wasser sind zwei abschließbare Unterkünfte eingeschoben. Wände und Dächer sind mit einer Lage rotem Gussbeton verkleidet. Sechzehn Stahlrohre stechen durch die Betonwände und geben den Blick frei auf Kanäle, Schornsteine, Bauernhöfe und Gasgewinnungsanlagen. Alle Gebäudeteile sind wie Module genormt. Die Veränderlichkeit des Observatoriums verweist auf den permanenten Wandel der Landschaft. Die roten Unterkünfte erinnern an die ursprüngliche Bodenhöhe in dieser Gegend, bevor der braunrote Torf abgegraben wurde. Die Paletten spiegeln das Erscheinungsbild des Gebietes aus der Vogelperspektive: langgestreckte Ländereien und Gräben, unterbrochen von Straßen und Kanälen.

Die Künstler beschlossen, die Verantwortung für die öffentliche Skulptur einer Privatperson zu übertragen, die das »Otium Leinewijk« nutzt sowie für Erhalt und Verwaltung sorgt. Es ist dem Verwalter überlassen, die Skulptur zu verändern oder zu erweitern. Natürlich darf er niemandem den Zugang verweigern, denn es handelt sich um ein öffentliches Kunstwerk in privater Obhut – Besucher und Verwalter besitzen also die gleichen Nutzungsrechte.

Observatorium inszeniert so Raum in der Öffentlichkeit – quasi öffentlichen Raum-Raum. Sie gestalten Raum nicht statisch, sondern formulieren die Verhältnismäßigkeit zwischen Raum und Gegenstand ebenso wie zwischen Betrachter und dem Feld seiner Betrachtung. Mit jedem der Observatorien verfolgt die Gruppe Observatorium die immer gleiche Absicht: den Betrachter des Kunstobjektes zum Betrachter seiner selbst zu machen. Wobei die Observatorien nicht, wie etwa die Spiegelpavillons eines Dan Graham, den Betrachter auf sich selbst zurückwerfen, sondern ihn quasi umfangen. Dass dabei die Umhausung die Identität des Betrachters, der ein Observatorium besucht, eher in Frage stellt als zum Ausdruck bringt, ist die Irritation, die aus den Observatorien zugleich das Gegenteil des Wunsches nach Heimat und Häuslichkeit werden lässt.

Die Gruppe Observatorium übergab die öffentliche Skulptur der Obhut einer Privatperson. Trotzdem können Reisende und Ruhesuchende die Unterkünfte in den Betonquadern nutzen.

The Observatorium group handed the public sculpture over to a private person who is to look after it. Travellers and passers-by wanting to rest there can still use the lodgings in the concrete boxes.

Die Südtangente in Holland

The "Zuidtangent" – the Southern Tangent in the Netherlands

Paul Kersten

Im Januar 2002 wurde das 22 Kilometer lange Kernstück der Südtangente eingeweiht. Die gesamte Trasse erstreckt sich über 78 Kilometer von IJmuiden nach Weesp, weitere Anschlüsse sind geplant. Damit wird die Südtangente zur längsten reinen Bustrasse der Welt. Nirgendwo sonst gibt es eine Busstrecke, auf der so schnell, komfortabel und zuverlässig gefahren werden kann – und das in einer der Gegenden der Niederlande mit den meisten Raumansprüchen. Die hohe Fahrtgeschwindigkeit ist nur möglich, weil die Strecke mit zahlreichen Tunnels, Aquädukten, Deichen und Brücken kreuzungsfrei angelegt wurde. Die Fahrbahn verläuft wie auf einer Achterbahn: mal 10 Meter runter, dann wieder 20 Meter hoch. In der topfebenen Polderlandschaft ist dies eine sensationelle Erfahrung. Die Haltestellen liegen häufig an Kreuzungen, wodurch sie meist erhöht und weithin sichtbar sind. Die expressive Gestaltung dieser Haltestellen steht in starkem Kontrast zur umgebenden Landschaft.

Das Konzept einer eigenen Busspur wurde in den Niederlanden in den neunziger Jahren erstmals für die Stadt Utrecht entwickelt. Die Einführung eines Schienensystems scheiterte dort nicht nur an den technischen Voraussetzungen, sondern insbesondere am schlechten Image der Straßenbahn und der damit verbundenen geringen Akzeptanz in der Bevölkerung. Statt des Light-rail-Konzepts wurde also als Alternative eine völlig freie Busspur entwickelt. Dieses System war, wie sich herausstellte, wesentlich flexibler, leichter zu integrieren und damit auch gesellschaftlich einfacher durchzusetzen. Auch für die Strecke der Südtangente war anfangs eine Light-rail-Verbindung geplant. Jedoch wurde bald klar, dass diese in den kommenden Jahrzehnten in der geplanten Größenordnung nicht rentabel wäre. Dennoch ist bei der Dimensionierung der gesamten Trasse darauf geachtet worden, dass der spätere Bau von Gleisen möglich ist, das heißt, die

Bunte Busunterstände sind Teil des Konzeptes der nur Bussen vorbehaltenen Verbindungsstrecke zwischen Schiphol und Haarlem.

Colourful bus stops are part of the concept for the dedicated bus route running between Schiphol and Haarlem.

In January 2002, the 22-kilometre-long main section of the Southern Tangent was opened to the public. The entire route is 78 kilometres long and connects IJmuiden with Weesp. Further extensions are planned, making the Southern Tangent the longest dedicated bus route in the world. Nowhere else, travelling by bus is as fast, comfortable and reliable – and this in one of Holland's regions with the highest spatial requirements. The high travelling speed is only possible because the route was planned with numerous tunnels, aqueducts, dykes and bridges, and without any crossings. Just like on a roller coaster, the lane descends by 10 metres only to quickly ascend again by 20 metres, quite a sensational experience in the flat polder landscape. Frequently, the bus stops are located at intersections so they are elevated and visible from a large distance. The expressive design of these bus stops contrast strongly with the surrounding landscape.

In the 1990s the concept of a dedicated bus lane was first developed for the city of Utrecht. In Utrecht, the introduction of a railway system failed not only due to the technical requirements but mainly due to the negative image of the tramway and the resulting low acceptance by the public. Thus, as an alternative to the light-rail concept, a completely separate bus track was developed. This system turned out to be more flexible and easier to integrate which in turn enhanced the chances of winning the public's approval. Originally, a light-rail connection was planned for the route of the Southern Tangent as well. Yet, it soon became clear that in the coming decades, a light-rail connection of this dimension would not have been profitable. Nevertheless, the route was designed to be converted for a probable future use by

Die Haltestellen der Bustrasse zwischen Amsterdam und Haarlem sollen neue Akzente im Bereich des öffentlichen Nahverkehrs setzen und diesem ein positives Image verleihen.

The bus stops along the bus route between Amsterdam and Haarlem are to add new highlights to the public transportation system and impart a positive image to the latter.

Schwarzer gegossener Kunststoff mit eingelassenen Mustern aus weißer Folie: Auch auf die Gestaltung des Bodenbelags wurde Wert gelegt.

Black cast plastic with integrated patterns made from white film: Importance was also attached to the design of the ground.

Trasse und die Haltestellen haben die gleichen Maße wie eine Schienenverbindung.

Das Büro VHP stedebouwkundigen + architecten + landschapsarchitecten aus Rotterdam hat in Zusammenarbeit mit dok industrial design den Entwurf für das Kernstück der Südtangente vorgelegt. Dieses verläuft vom Amsterdamer Flughafen Schiphol über Hoofddorp bis nach Haarlem. Sowohl die Bahn, als auch die Haltestellen und die direkte Umgebung sollten Qualität ausstrahlen. So sind alle Haltestellen behindertengerecht zugänglich und wo nötig mit Aufzügen ausgestattet. Die 75 Meter langen Bahnsteige wurden um 30 Zentimeter angehoben, um ebenerdiges Einsteigen zu ermöglichen. An den Haltestellen gibt es abschließbare Einstellplätze für Fahrräder und eine 30 Meter lange gläserne Bahnsteigüberdachung mit Windschutz. Der Sicherheit zuliebe sind die Bahnsteige gut beleuchtet und übersichtlich gestaltet. Ein elektronisches Anzeigesystem gibt exakt an, wann der nächste Bus kommt und übersichtliche Infotafeln versorgen die Reisenden mit den übrigen Informationen. Neben der Trasse selbst wurde auch die unmittelbare Umgebung in die Planung einbezogen. Wo erforderlich, wurden selbst große Verkehrsadern vollständig umgebaut, wie etwa die Van Heuven Goedhartlaan in Hoofddorp. Hier wurden etwa 700 fünfzehnjährige Platanen, die wegen der Bauarbeiten weichen mussten, in ein Depot gebracht und später wieder gepflanzt. Eingriffe in die Umgebung wurden so weit wie möglich vermieden, für Grünflächen und Wasserläufe, die die neue Trasse durchschneidet, wurden neue Planungen erstellt.

Ausgangspunkt bei der Gestaltung der Baukörper war der Kontrast zwischen einer schweren Basis und einem leichten Oberbau. Farb- und Materialwahl sollen diesen Kontrast verstärken. Die Fahrbahn selbst wurde als »dynamische Ebene« aufgefasst, als eine auf- und abrollende Fahrbahn. Alles was sich unter dieser Ebene abspielt, gehört zur Grundfläche der Bahn

tram or light rail which means that road and bus stops are of the same dimensions as a railway track.

Together with dok industrial design, the architectural bureau VHP stedebouwkundigen + architecten + landschapsarchitecten from Rotterdam submitted the design for the main section of the Southern Tangent. It runs from the Amsterdam Schiphol Airport via Hoofddorp to Haarlem. The traffic lane, the bus stops as well as the surrounding area should communicate quality. The bus stops are accessible for physically challenged people and equipped with elevators where necessary. The 75-metre platform was raised by 30 centimetres to allow access at ground level. All bus stops are equipped with lockable cycle racks and boast a 30-metre long glass roof with additional wind protection. For security reasons, the platforms are well lit and have an uncluttered and open design. An electronic display system indicates the arrival of the next bus and user-friendly information boards provide travellers with other valuable information. The immediate surroundings of the bus lane were also included in the design plans. Wherever necessary, even main roads were entirely reconstructed, such as the Van Heuven Goedhartlaan in Hoofddorp. Here, about seven hundred 15-year-old plane trees were moved to a depot during the road construction work to be replanted after the work had been completed. Intrusions upon the natural environment were avoided as much as possible. New plans were drawn up for all green spaces and watercourses the new route runs through.

The design concept for the structures was the contrast between a solid base and a light superstructure; the choice of colour and material are to intensify this contrast. The bus lane itself was seen as a "dynamic level", as a roll-on/roll-off

Zuidtangent, main section, The Netherlands
Client: Province of Noord-Holland
Planners: VHP stedebouwkundigen + architecten + landschapsarchitecten bv, Rotterdam
and dok industrial design, Amsterdam
Designteam: Paul Kersten, Ron Klein Breteler, Maurice Nio, Gijs Ockoloen, Germaine Sanders
Planning and construction: 1998 – 2002
Costs: 20 Million Euro

lane. Everything below this level belongs to the base of the road with its rather rough construction. The world above this level is blooming. The bus stops with their expressive design and strikingly coloured roofs resemble flowers coming into bloom and also call to mind the "Floriade". This horticultural exhibition – the world's largest and held once every ten years – was opened to the public at the same time as the Southern Tangent, the latter serving as a direct connection between airport and the Floriade.

With the Southern Tangent, the designers tried to improve the negative image of the bus stops by aesthetic means. The Southern Tangent was to attract attention, stand out, seduce and have a completely different appearance than the ordinary bus stops with their gloomy shelters, concrete slab floors and the post with the yellow sign offering almost undecipherable information on the route. Travelling by bus on the Southern Tangent, on the other hand, is supposed to be cool, the short stop at the bus stop (a bus arrives every 7 minutes on the dot) should not be a punishment to the travellers but an event – and the bus ride is to be a thrilling adventure. Thus, the design is part of the marketing concept that the number of passengers should increase as a result of the improved image.

For the planners, the qualities of use of the bus system were as important as the quality for residents and passers-by. Thus, the bus route with its bus stops was not shielded from the surrounding area by any means, but instead became a clearly visible, integral part of the new public space. At every bus stop open spaces were created which connect the bus stop with the surrounding area. Depending on location and specification, their appearance varies.

mit ihrer eher rohen Konstruktion. Die Welt über dieser Ebene blüht. Die expressiv geformten Haltestellen mit ihren auffallend eingefärbten Dächern sprießen wie Blumen in der Fahrbahn und geben hiermit auch einen Hinweis auf die Floriade. Diese, alle zehn Jahre stattfindende, »größte Blumenschau der Welt« wurde gleichzeitig mit der Südtangente eröffnet, die für die Floriade als direkter Flughafenzubringer diente.

Bei der Südtangente wurde die Ästhetik von den Entwerfern als Mittel eingesetzt, um das negative Image von Bushaltestellen umzukrempeln. Die Südtangente sollte auffallen, verführen und eine ganz andere Ausstrahlung haben, als die bekannten Bushaltestellen mit ihrem düsteren Unterstand, dem Betonplattenboden und dem Pfosten mit gelbem Schild, dem nur mit viel Mühe die Route entlockt werden kann. Das Reisen auf der Südtangente dagegen sollte cool sein, der kurze Aufenthalt – pünktlich alle sieben Minuten kommt ein Bus – an der Haltestelle keine Strafe, sondern ein Erlebnis und die Fahrt selbst aufregend. Die Gestaltung ist somit Teil des Marketingkonzepts, das über das verbesserte Image die Fahrgastzahlen steigern soll.

Die Nutzungsqualitäten des Bussystems waren den Planern ebenso wichtig wie die Qualität für Anwohner und Passanten. Die Bustrasse und ihre Haltestellen wurden also nicht mit allen Mitteln von der Umgebung abgeschirmt, sondern sind ein deutlich sichtbarer Bestandteil des neuen öffentlichen Raums. An allen Haltestellen wurden Plätze angelegt, die die Haltestelle mit der Umgebung verknüpfen. Je nach Ort und Anforderungsprofil sehen sie immer etwas anders aus.

Die Kernstrecke verfügt über 15 Haltestellen, die sich alle voneinander unterscheiden. Durch ihre verschiedenen Farben und das unterschiedliche Zebrastreifenmuster auf den Bahnsteigen und Vorplätzen variiert auch ihr Erscheinungsbild in der Umgebung. Die Umsteigepunkte heben sich nochmals durch eine größere Überdachung und einen von drei auf vier Meter verbreiterten Bahnsteig von den anderen Haltestellen ab. Der Name der Haltestellen ist wie eine Grafik in die langen gläsernen Windschirme gedruckt. Hierdurch erhalten die Haltestellen ihre eigene erkennbare Identität. Das gewählte Entwurfsprinzip verträgt Nuancierung, ohne dadurch an Kraft einzubüßen. Jede einzelne Haltestelle hat ihr abgestecktes Territorium, das offen, übersichtlich und in den Abendstunden lichtdurchflutet ist.

In der Entwurfsphase wurde viel mit für den öffentlichen Raum ungewöhnlichen Materialien experimentiert. So wurden bei den Dächern doppelt gebogene Glasscheiben eingesetzt, zwischen die von Hand Farbe

Die gläsernen Bahnsteigüberdachungen mit Windschutz sind neue Merkpunkte in der flachen Polderlandschaft. Sie signalisieren einen neuen öffentlichen Raum.
The glass platform roofs with wind protection provide new focal points in the flat polder landscape. They indicate a new public space and characterize the surrounding area.

Das Kernstück der Bustrasse wurde anlässlich der Floriade Haarlemmermeer 2002 eröffnet. Die bunten Glasdächer mit ihrer expressiven Form sind eine Hommage an die Blumenschau.

The main section of the bus route was opened to the public on the occasion of the 2002 Floriade Haarlemmermeer. The colourful glass roofs with their expressive forms are an homage to the horticultural exhibition.

In 1998 it was awarded the "European Public Transport Price" – a European prize awarded every two years to promising and innovative projects relating to the public transportation system.

The central route has 15 bus stops that all differ from one another. Due to their different colours and the zebra-pattern on the platforms and open spaces, their appearance also varies from the surrounding area. The interchange stations themselves stand out from the other bus stops thanks to a larger roof and a platform, widened from 3 to 4 metres. The name of the bus stops is imprinted on the long glass wind panels like a graphic work of art.

It is in this manner that the bus stops gain their unique, recognizable identity. The chosen design principle can tolerate subtle changes without forfeiting any of its strength. Each bus stop has its own defined territory that is open, visually accessible and light-flooded in the evenings.

During the draft stage materials were tested that are quite uncommon for the use in public spaces. Such as for instance the roofs that are made of doubly curved glass panes, in between which colour was sprayed by hand. Each glass pane has its own cloud pattern, making it one of its kind. The platform surface consists of black cast plastic into which a striped zebra-pattern made of white film is integrated. The guiding strips for the blind are made out of glass beads and the yellow marking lines were cast into the ground. In front of the bus stops, a concrete pavement was installed with surfaces in five different shades of colour – exclusively developed for the Southern Tangent. The furniture on the platforms and the open spaces surrounding them and also at the cycle racks was specially designed for the Southern Tangent.

For each bus stop an individual lighting plan was developed. A square with 12 metre high lampposts illuminates the surrounding area. Fluorescent lamp tubes below the glass roofs illuminate the platforms, which are a spectacular sight at night.

aufgesprüht wurde. Jede Glasscheibe hat ihr eigenes Wolkenmuster und ist somit einzigartig. Die Oberfläche der Bahnsteige besteht aus schwarzem, gegossenem Kunststoff, in den mit weißer Folie helle Zebrasteifen eingelassen wurden. Die Blinden-Führungsstreifen sind aus Glasperlen und die Markierungslinien wurden mit gelber Farbe in den Belag eingegossen. Vor den Haltestellen wurde ein eigens für die Südtangente entwickeltes Betonpflaster mit Oberflächen in fünf verschiedenen Farbtönen verlegt. Auch das Mobiliar auf den Bahnsteigen und Vorplätzen, sowie bei den Fahrradständern wurde speziell für die Südtangente entworfen.

Für jede Haltestelle wurde ein eigener Beleuchtungsplan erstellt. Ein Karree mit zwölf Meter hohen Lichtmasten leuchtet das Gelände aus. Leuchtstoffröhren unter den Glasdächern beleuchten die Bahnsteige, die abends einen spektakulären Anblick bieten.

Die Details der einzelnen Haltestellen wurden sorgfältig ausformuliert: Die Blinden-Führungsstreifen sind aus Glasperlen, die Markierungen heben sich mit ihrem starken Gelb vom Asphalt ab. Alle Haltestellen wurden behindertengerecht gestaltet, wo nötig, stehen zusätzlich gläserne Aufzüge zur Verfügung.

Great importance was attached to the detail work of the bus stops. The guiding strips for the blind are made from glass beads and the bright yellow of the marking lines stands out against the asphalt. The bus stops are accessible for physically challenged people and are – where necessary – additionally equipped with glass elevators.

Pavillons im Botanischen Garten von Meran

Pavilions in the Botanical Garden of Trauttmansdorff Castle in Merano

»Le monde est plus petit, sans fou – Die Welt wäre ärmer ohne Verrückte.« Eine Aussage, die auf die Folies, die Pavillons in den Gärten von Schloss Trauttmansdorff in Meran zutreffend sein könnte. Kann Natur überhaupt künstlerisch dargestellt werden?

Wenn Claude Cézanne bereits am Ende des 19. Jahrhunderts erkannt hat: »Man muss sich beeilen, wenn man noch etwas sehen will, alles verschwindet« und damit meinte, dass sich alles stets ändert, dass Natur nicht dargestellt werden kann, ohne das Licht und innere Zusammenhänge in Betracht zu ziehen und bemerkte, dass in dem Moment, in dem der erste Pinselstrich gesetzt wird, erkannte Tatsachen schon wieder verschwunden sind, um wie viel mehr muss man sich wundern, dass in Meran diese Momentaufnahme nicht nur malerisch versucht wurde, sondern auch noch gebaut. So sind Orte entstanden, die einladen wollen zum Innehalten und Verweilen, sich einzulassen auf Farbenspiel und die natürliche stets vorhandene Veränderung, welche auch dann stattfindet, wenn wir sie nicht sehen können. Orte deren Reiz darin liegt, das Unmögliche zu versuchen, um so zu Vermittlern zu werden zwischen gewachsener Natürlichkeit und gebauter Künstlichkeit.

Margit Klammer

Ein botanischer Garten ist keine natürlich gewachsene Landschaft, sondern ein künstlich geschaffener Raum. Natur allein würde keine Bereiche erstellen, eingeteilt in Sonnen-, Terrassen-, Wasser- und Waldgärten. Die Konturen würden verschwimmen und die Pflanzen würden sich ihren natürlichen Standort selbst suchen.

Um diese Themengärten den Besuchern näher zu bringen, entstand der Wunsch, die künstlich erstellten Bereiche in Gestalt von Pavillons, in eine für jedermann nachvollziehbare Formensprache zu übertragen, kleine sinnliche Ereignisse zu schaffen und zu ausdrucksstarken, für alle Sinne wahrnehmbaren Erscheinungsbildern zu verdichten. Sie sollten Art und Wesen der sie umgebenden Pflanzen sichtbar machen, erklären woher sie stammen und welche Lebensbedingungen sie brauchen.

Entstanden sind Konglomerate, angesiedelt zwischen Kunst und Architektur, im Einklang und als Kontrapunkt zur gewachsenen Natur, als dichte Packung von Kommunikation zwischen Mensch und Pflanze; nicht nur Skulptur und nicht ausschließlich dem Witterungs-

Geheimnisse der Pflanzen – Folies, die den Besuchern wissenschaftliche Informationen anders als gewohnt vermitteln.

The secrets of plants – Follies that provide visitors with a wide range of scientific information in a quite unusual way.

"Le monde est plus petit, sans fou – the world would be less without fools." A statement that could apply to the pavilions in the gardens of the Trauttmansdorff Castle in Merano. Can nature actually be portrayed in an artistic way?

At the end of the 19th century, Claude Cézanne had already realized: "One has to hurry, if one still wants to catch sight of things; everything is disappearing", implying that everything is constantly changing and that nature cannot be depicted without considering the light and the internal context. He noticed that at the very moment of applying the first brush stroke to an empty canvas, earlier realizations have already vanished.

All the more surprising is the attempt in Merano to capture a single moment not only on canvas but in constructed pavilions. Hence places were developed that invite us to pause, linger and allow us to surrender to the play of colours and the constant natural change that exists even when we don't see it.

Places that are appealing, because they try to do the impossible and thus become mediators between grown naturalness and constructed artificiality. A botanical garden is not a naturally grown landscape but an artificially created space. Nature itself would not create areas divided into gardens of sun, terrace, water, and forest. Contours would blend and plants would choose their own natural habitat.

To give the visitors a better understanding of these theme parks, the desire arose to translate the pavilions – artificially constructed areas – into forms that would be comprehensible to everyone, to create small sensuous events and to condense them to an expressive appearance, perceptible to all senses. The pavilions were to make visible the type and character of the plants surrounding them, to explain their origin and living conditions. The result were conglomerates, somewhere in between art and architecture, in harmony and as a counterpart to grown nature, as a tight bundle of communication between man and plant; jewels in a garden, serving neither solely as a sculpture nor solely to provide information or shelter from the weather.

And what finally induced the desire to give a home even to animals in this botanical garden, to create an aviary with room for birds and people? A pavilion that raises the question: "Who is imprisoned and who is free?" A world was to be created, complete and comprehending life as a whole.

Seemingly separate and diverse natural microcosms merge and are accessible through art and architecture. Animals more than plants contribute to our feeling like equals among equals. Protecting diversity, giving it space and redefining ourselves in this space may be sheer foolishness and the purpose of the follies. A crazy world, a world whose parameters have been shifted and redefined, in which our eyes are opened up to differences and thus, in the end, we are certain that only the art of posing questions differentiates us from other beings.

It is through form and material that the pavilions try to answer questions: why don't water lilies drown and why do cactuses prick? What enables plants of the Mediterranean region survive in heat and dryness and how did exotic plants find their way to our continent? Everything is flowing, caused by growth and decay just as day follows night and spring succeeds winter.

Constructing visible and tangible ephemeral things, seemingly making them resistant to change, is comparable to freezing a moment in time and reflects our desire for something con-

schutz und der Information dienende Kleinode in der Landschaft. Und was war schließlich ausschlaggebend, dass selbst Tiere Platz fanden, in diesem botanischen Garten und der Wunsch entstand eine Voliere zu schaffen mit Platz für Vögel und Menschen? Ein Pavillon, der die Frage aufwirft »Wer ist gefangen und wer ist frei?« Eine Welt sollte entstehen, die umfassend ist und Leben als Ganzes versteht.

Scheinbar getrennte, verschieden natürliche Welten gehen ineinander über und werden durch Kunst und Architektur zugänglich gemacht. Tiere tragen, eher noch als Pflanzen, dazu bei, uns als Gleiche zu verstehen unter Gleichen. Die Vielfalt zu schützen, ihr Raum zu geben und uns in diesem Raum neu zu definieren, mag Wahnsinn sein und Aufgabe der Follies. Eine verrückte Welt, eine Welt in der Parameter verschoben werden und neu definiert, in der die Augen geöffnet werden für das Andere, wodurch wir letztendlich die Gewissheit erhalten, dass uns nur die Kunst Fragen zu stellen von anderen Lebewesen unterscheidet.

Unterschiedlich gestaltete Follies widmen sich im Botanischen Garten von Schloss Trauttmansdorff in Meran einzelnen botanischen Aspekten. Doch auch zur Bewunderung der eindrücklichen Natur Südtirols werden die Besucher aufgefordert.

Differently shaped follies in the Botanical Garden of Trauttmansdorff Castle in Merano devote themselves to individual botanical aspects. The visitors are invited to admire South Tyrol's impressive nature as well.

Jedem einzelnen der insgesamt elf Pavillons liegt eine spezielle Gestaltung zu Grunde. Mit der Voliere, einem runden Drahtgerüst, in dessen zentralem Raum sich Vögel und Menschen gleichzeitig aufhalten, werden auch Tiere als Teil der Natur in die Gestaltung miteinbezogen.
(Konzept: Margit Klammer)

Every single one of the eleven pavilions has a special design concept. With the aviary, a round wire structure with a central space shared by people and birds at the same time, animals are integrated into the design as part of nature.
(Design: Margit Klammer)

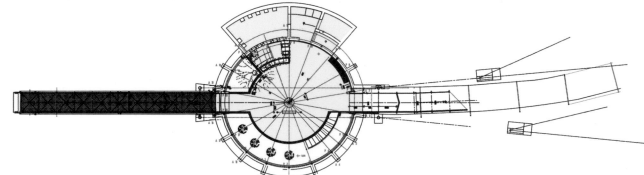

Unterschiedliche Aspekte der Botanik greifen die weiteren Folies auf. Der Pavillon Flaumeichenwald (oben links) widerspiegelt durch die Reduktion auf wenige Materialien die harten Lebensbedingungen dieser Pflanzengesellschaft. Das Licht- und Schattenspiel des Pavillons Sommergrüner Laubwald (unten links), versucht die spezielle Atmosphäre eines Laubwaldes einzufangen. Der Herbstpavillon als weiteres Beispiel widmet sich dem Thema des Vergehens und zeigt die Natur im Herbst.
(Konzept Pavillons Flaumeichenwald und Sommergrüner Laubwald: SSS Schweiz, Konzept Herbstpavillon: Margit Klammer)

The other follies pick up on different aspects of botany. Reduced to but a few materials, the pavilion Pubescent Oak Forest (top, left) reflects the harsh living conditions of this plant community. The play of light and shadow of the pavilion Summer Green Deciduous Forest (bottom, left) tries to capture the characteristic atmosphere of a deciduous forest. The Autumn Pavilion, as another example, devotes itself to the topic of gradual decay and illustrates nature in autumn.
(Design pavilions Pubescent Oak Forest and Summer Green Deciduous Forest: SSS Switzerland, design Autumn Pavilion: Margit Klammer)

Durch Form und Material versuchen die Pavillons Antworten zu geben auf Fragen: Warum gehen Seerosen nicht unter und weshalb stechen Kakteen? Was befähigt die Pflanzen der mediterranen Zone in Hitze und Trockenheit zu überleben oder wie kamen exotische Pflanzen zu uns? Alles ist im Fluss, bedingt durch Werden und Vergehen, wie der Tag die Nacht ablöst und das Frühjahr den Winter.

Unserem Bedürfnis nach einer Konstante, nach Statik in dynamischen Zeiten wurde aber nur insofern Rechnung getragen, als das sichtbare und greifbare Erbauen ephemerer Dinge, welche dadurch nur scheinbar keinem Wandel mehr unterworfen sind, einem Einfrieren von Tatsachen gleichkommt. Indem versucht wird, Unsichtbares sichtbar zu machen, sich stets Wandelndes festzuhalten und Atmosphären aus dem Inneren der Pflanzen zu erzeugen, wird ein Zugang geöffnet, der eine offene Betrachtungsweise ermöglicht. Der Reiz lag darin, gerade das Unkontrollierbare in kontrollierbare Formen zu übertragen, um sich hinterher der Relativität der Wahrnehmung bewusst zu werden. Eine Wahrnehmung, die sich im alltäglichen Leben meist auf Augen und Kopf konzentriert, hier aber alle Sinne ansprechen soll. Denn wie viel mehr könnten wir wahrnehmen, wenn unsere Sinne so ausgeprägt wären, wie jene der Pflanzen und wir deren spezielle Fähigkeiten hätten, die ihnen Leben und Überleben sichern, in Sommer und Winter, bei Kälte und Hitze.

Damit wird die Suche nach den Formen, die Natur darstellen sollen, aber auch eine Suche nach Zeit. Es gibt keine eindeutigen, ständigen und unwandelbaren Eigenschaften und Formen, nur Interpretationen des Sichtbaren. Die Pavillons entspringen somit unserem Willen, festhalten zu wollen, was ist.

So sind die gebauten Utopien dieses Gartens der Versuch einer Annäherung an eine Natur, die wir wohl nie ganz begreifen werden. Sie machen uns bewusst dass auch wir Menschen dem Wandel der Zeit ausgeliefert sind. Nicht anders als Pflanzen. Auch treten sie den Beweis dafür an, dass Natur viel mehr ist als ihre Darstellung. Deshalb sind sie nötig, um Orte der Betrachtung zu schaffen und uns die Augen zu öffnen. Pavillons im herkömmlichen Sinn wären dagestanden in reiner Funktion und keine Annäherung hätte stattgefunden zwischen Kultur und Natur. So sind sie alle anders und werden bereits von weitem zu jenem Identifikationssymbol für den Bereich, den sie beschreiben, und zum Zielpunkt auf unserem Spaziergang durch den Garten.

stant, something stable in dynamic times. By trying to make the invisible visible, to constantly capture changing things and to create atmospheres from the inside of plants, a door is opened to a broader view of things.

The challenge was to convert the uncontrollable to a controllable form, only to realize the relativity of perception afterwards. A perception that is usually reduced to sight and mind in everyday life, but here is to appeal to all senses. And how much more could we perceive if our senses were as well-developed as those of plants, and if we had their special abilities that allow them to live and survive during the summer as well as in the wintertime, in cold and heat.

Thus the search for forms that can present nature also becomes a search for time. There are no clear, constant and immutable characteristics and forms, only interpretations of the visible. Pavilions therefore spring from our intention to capture what exists at this very moment. Thus the constructed utopias in this garden are an effort to approximate a form of nature we will probably never fully understand. They make us realize that human beings are subject to the change of time as well – just as plants are. In addition, they offer evidence that nature is much more than its portrayal. They are necessary to create places of perception and make us become aware. Pavilions in their conventional meaning would have been standing there in their pure functional meaning, and no approach between culture and nature would have taken place. Hence they are all different from each other and even from a large distance they become a symbol of identification for the place they describe and the final destination of our stroll through the garden.

Folies im Parco di Casvegno in Mendrisio

Green follies in Parco di Casvegno, Mendrisio

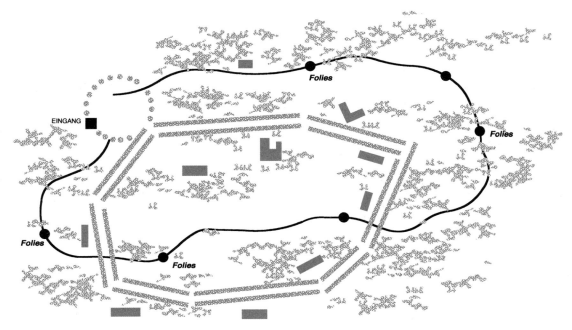

The goal of the project for Parco di Casvegno in Mendrisio, Italy, was to upgrade part of the grounds of a neuropsychiatric clinic and make the park accessible for nearby residents. Being located close to unattractive clinic buildings, the park was associated with illness and sadness, and thus one of the objectives of the project was to make it a place of joy, peace and reflection. This has been achieved in part with playful design elements in the form of green follies. Made of trees and shrubs, they play a key role in lightening the character of the park and at the same time make it a pleasant place to be, one conducive to thought and reflection.

Before the project took place, the 30-hectare park had a remarkable stock of trees and bushes. Yet although they stood in close relationship with their surroundings, they were not arranged in structures of design value. Rather, the trees had been planted, transplanted and felled for many years according to forest management principles.

The new design is built up around a new footpath that leads around the whole site, devised to enable a journey of discovery through the vegetation of the 19th-century park. The purpose of the path, which is executed with minimal means, is to entertain the people who stroll along it, to awaken their curiosity and encourage reverie - some of the processes that are set in mention when people discover a new place, such as a town or an old garden, or when they gaze at a landscape, or become absorbed in a narrative or a piece of music. People wandering through the Sacro Bosco, the sacred wood at Villa Orsini in Bomarzo, still experience "wonder and amazement", four hundred years after it was created, and visitors to the 19th-century Parco Durazzo Pallavicini, near Genua, find that "imaginary stories in pictures and acts" begin to

Ziel des Projektes für den Parco di Casvegno in Mendrisio war es, den Park der Neuropsychiatrischen Klinik aufzuwerten und ihn für die Anwohner zugänglich zu machen. Aus einem Ort in der Nähe wenig attraktiver Klinikbauten, der aufgrund seiner Lage mit Traurigkeit und Krankheit assoziiert wurde, sollte ein Park entstehen, der zu Freude, Ruhe, Gelassenheit und Besinnung animiert. Die in die Gestaltung integrierten Folies aus lebender Pflanzensubstanz tragen dazu bei: Als spielerische Gestaltungselemente sind sie sozusagen der Schlüssel für die Öffnung des Parks, für seine fröhliche und besinnliche Erschließung. Das 30 Hektar große Gelände weist einen bemerkenswerten Gehölzbestand auf, der in enger Beziehung zur Umgebung steht. Vor der Neugestaltung der Parkanlage waren keine besonderen Strukturen mit gestalterischem Wert vorhanden. Jahrelang hatte man nach forstwirtschaftlichen Konzepten Bäume gepflanzt, umgepflanzt und gefällt.

Das Projekt baut auf einem neuen Fußweg auf, der das gesamte Parkgelände umläuft. Dieser neue Weg ist als eine Entdeckungsreise durch die Vegetation des im 19. Jahrhundert angelegten

Paolo L. Bürgi

Gewachsene Folies werden sich im Laufe der Zeit verändern und die Besucher immer wieder mit neuen Bildern überraschen.

Structures made up of trees and shrubs will change in appearance with the passing of time and provide visitors with ever-new surprises.

Ein neuer Fußweg ermöglicht einen Rundgang durch den Park der Neuropsychiatrischen Klinik in Mendrisio. Daran aufgereiht liegen die sechs aus Pflanzen bestehenden Folies.

A new footpath is now to lead around the whole of the park at the neuropsychiatric clinic in Mendrisio, passing six follies made up of trees and shrubs on its way.

Parks entworfen. Der mit minimalen Mitteln realisierte Weg soll die darauf Wandelnden belustigen, ihre Neugierde wecken und zum Träumen anregen. Dies sind einige der Empfindungen, die bei der Entdeckung eines Ortes, einer Stadt, eines alten Gartens, bei der Betrachtung einer Landschaft oder beim Eintauchen in eine Erzählung, in ein Musikstück und ein Abenteuer wahrgenommen werden können. »Wunder und Bewunderung« sind es, die uns noch heute, nach vier Jahrhunderten, im heiligen Wald von Bomarzo begleiten. Es ist die »imaginäre Erzählung in Bildern und Akten«, die wir noch heute in dem Park Durazzo-Pallavicini aus dem 19. Jahrhundert nahe Genua erleben. Dies sind nur zwei von vielen Beispielen. Die Besucher des Parco di Casvegno in Mendrisio können entlang des Weges verschiedene Folies entdecken – einfache, die Besucher amüsierende Pflanzenobjekte. Wie in Barock und Renaissance, Zeitepochen, während derer Vergnügen, Wunder, Komik und Freude eine wichtige Rolle spielten, hat der Baum in den Folies eine spielerische Bedeutung. Sie greifen ein Jahrhunderte altes Motiv der Gartenkunst wieder auf, das von trompe-l'œil bis zu Blickfängen reicht. Die einzig und allein aus Bäumen und Sträuchern bestehenden Folies sind als sehr einfache, fast asketische Objekte gedacht. Vielleicht liegt dies daran, dass ich überzeugt davon bin, dass sich gerade in der Schlichtheit

unfold as they walk around it. And this is to mention just two examples from among many.

Accordingly, visitors to Parco di Casvegno in Mendrisio come across various green follies as they progress along the path – simple plant structures designed to amuse and divert. During the Baroque and Renaissance ages, eras in which tricks and wonders, enjoyment and pleasure played an important role, trees were of playful significance in the garden follies of the time. Accordingly, the green follies at Parco di Casvegno refer back to a centuries-old garden design feature, one that ranged from trompe-l'œils to eye-catchers. In contrast, however, they solely consist of trees and shrubs, and are simple, even ascetic objects. Maybe this is because I take the viewpoint that the art of leaving things out and finding the essential is a matter of simplicity. This is also an ethical consideration, particularly when you consider how much modern-day art is unable to resist the temptations of hedonism, prevailing fashions and the need to consume. As a reflection of the times that produce them, landscapes have also become objects to be consumed, and in this respect are not seen as any different from other areas of scenery. Consumed today, discarded tomorrow. This situation is summed up by Oscar Wilde's pithy remark: "We are living in an era in which the superfluous is our only necessity".

The inaccessible place. At this folly, fastigiate oaks are planted so close to each other that their trunks will meet one day, creating a closed circle that visitors will no longer be able to enter. This state will not come about for many decades, but in the meantime it is hoped that the experimental folly will encourage visitors to reflect on modern man's relationship to time: i.e. acceptance of the rhythms of nature in contrast to the uncer-

Der unterschiedliche Habitus der verwendeten Pflanzen verstärkt den Charakter der Folies: In einem Kreis gepflanzte Säuleneichen lassen eine Lichtung frei, die im Laufe der Zeit nicht mehr betretbar sein wird (Seite 38 oben), hochstämmige Steineichen bilden ein dunkles Baumquadrat (Seite 38 unten) und schlanke Zypressen gewähren in Reihen gepflanzt immer neue Perspektiven.

The differing growth forms of the plants underscore the character of the green follies: fastigiate oaks planted in a circle will one day form an impenetrable glade (top opposite); tall standard evergreen oaks planted in a grid create the impression of a dark cube of trees (bottom opposite), while the rows of slender cypresses (above) create different perspective illusions.

das Wesentliche und die Kunst des Weglassen entdecken lassen. Dies ist ein ethischer Aspekt, wenn man bedenkt, wie viele der heutigen Kunstwerke sich den Verlockungen des Hedonismus, des Konsums und den herrschenden aktuellen Moden unterwerfen. Die Landschaft, Abbild der aktuellen Situation und Zeit, wird mitunter zum Konsumobjekt, das mit anderen über einen Kamm geschert wird. Heute wird es konsumiert, morgen hat es schon nicht mehr denselben Wert. Eine Situation, die die Worte des Schriftstellers Oscar Wilde mit extremer Klarheit beschreiben: »Wir leben in einer Epoche, in der das Überflüssige unsere einzige Notwendigkeit ist.«

Der unerreichbare Ort. In einem kleinen geschlossenen Kreis (»cerchio chiuso«) gepflanzte Säuleneichen sind so dicht nebeneinander platziert, dass sich ihre Stämme eines Tages berühren werden. Dadurch wird den Besuchern der Zugang zu der umschlossenen Fläche einmal verwehrt werden. Während dieses vorgesehene Ziel erst in einigen Jahrzehnten erreicht werden wird, soll dieses Folie mit experimentellem Charakter vielleicht einen Impuls für die Reflexion über die Zeit und unsere Beziehung zur Zeit geben können: die Akzeptanz von Rhythmen, die von der Natur vorgegeben sind, im Gegensatz zur Unsicherheit und Eile der Gegenwart. Die Eiche, Quercus robur, ist mit ihrer Langlebigkeit über mehrere Jahrhunderte und ihrem in dem Adjektiv »robur« zum Ausdruck kommenden harten Holz ein symbolträchtiger Baum mediterraner Kultur. Die Varietät ‘Pyramidalis’ wird durch ihren besonderen Habitus charakterisiert.

Die Baumkathedrale, der Säulengarten. Hochstämmige immergrüne Steineichen sind in einem Raster gepflanzt, so dass sie ein dunkles »Baumquadrat« (»quadrato d'alberi«) bilden. Sie fassen einen Raum in der Landschaft. Ihre Kronen erscheinen wie ein quadratisches Volumen auf Säulen. Der Besucher wird auf dieses ordentliche Raster aufmerksam und verlangsamt seinen Schritt. Das quadratische Raster lädt ein, einzutreten und zwischen den Baumstämmen hindurchzuschauen. Auf dem Erdboden entsteht ein dichter Teppich trockenen Laubes. Die Steineiche, Quercus ilex, ist eine typische Baumart der mediterranen Macchia. Sie wächst langsam und kann bis zu drei Jahrhunderte alt werden. Seit der Antike ist sie viel beachtet und von Dichtern besungen.

Das perspektivische Bühnenbild, die Illusion. Zypressen sind beidseitig entlang einer Achse gepflanzt und erzeugen eine »falsche Perspektive« (»falsa prospettiva«), das heißt eine optische Täuschung. In der Achse stehend, hat der Besucher zwei unterschiedliche Blicke, die überraschen und auf verschiedene Art Beziehungen zum Park aufbauen. Es handelt sich um ein Spiel mit einer

Green follies in Parco di Casvegno, Mendrisio
Client: Governo del Cantone Ticino
Landscape architect: Paolo L. Bürgi
Concept: 1987
Construction: 1989 – 1996

tainy and haste of the present. The oak, Quercus robur, lives for several centuries and thus stands for longevity, while the hardness of its wood is expressed by the robur in its botanical name. It is thus a highly symbolical tree in the culture of the Mediterranean, whereby the Pyramidalis variety is characterised by its particular form of growth.

The cathedral of trees, the fastigiate garden. Tall standard evergreen oaks are planted in a grid layout to form a dark square of trees, a quadrangular-shaped element that creates the overall appearance of a cube standing on columns. The visitor, noticing this formal arrangement, slows down his step and walking up to it, feels drawn to enter the square and move between the trees. Eventually, the ground between the trunks will be covered with a thick carpet of dry leaves. The evergreen oak, Quercus ilex, is a typical trees species of the Mediterranean macchia underbrush. As such it grows slowly, and can reach three hundred years in age. Accordingly, it has been an object of respect since the days of Antiquity, its praises often sung by poets.

The perspective view, the illusion. In this folly, cypresses are planted on either side of an imaginary line, creating a false perspective or prospect, in other words, an optical illusion. Depending on which direction the visitors looks when standing between the rows, he gains two different impressions, both offering a surprising effect and both standing in relationship to the park in their differing ways. The matter in hand is a *trompe-l'œil* in the third dimension. When looked at in the one direction, the cypresses, which are planted at exact distances along two converging lines, create a feeling of depth. This impression is underscored by the slightly rising ground and the dark background formed by a group of imposing copper beeches. A look in the other direction yields a different impression, one in which the trees run down the slope in perfectly parallel lines, thus involving no suggestion of spatial depth. This effect is caused by the lack of a vanishing point in the open view, and is underscored by the nearby presence of a solitary conifer. The cypress, Cupressus sempervirens, one of the most important cultivated tree species since Antiquity, is a symbol of the flame, female beauty and death, but also of longevity. In fact, it is said that cypresses over a thousand years of age are still in existence.

The place of pleasure and diversion. A "frivolous wood" made up of hundreds of hornbeams forms an island in the existing vegetation. The more it grows, the more the grove will enable differing perspectives and viewlines and become a garden for playing hide and seek, although the straight paths will be stopped short by dense undergrowth one day. This idea of a grove is part of a concept I once suggested for a new municipal park. The paths that run through it are laid out in such a way that they constantly confront visitors with new situations, forcing them to choose between paths and thus make new discoveries. The etymology of Carpinus in Carpinus betulus (hornbeam) is unknown, but of all the possible roots, I would like to quote the Celtic one, which yields *car* (wood) and *pin* (head). These terms refer to the use of the wood for games, i.e. "gamewood". Hornbeams are small trees, remnants of the undergrowth of large and ancient forests.

The invented, the surreal. A row of fastigiate hornbeams in high tapered shapes traces a twisted longitudinal axis, resulting in a *torsione vegetale*, a surreal plant sculpture. Planted in a close

perspektivischen Illusion, um ein trompe-l'œil in der dritten Dimension. Von der einen Seite betrachtet erzeugen die in genau ermittelten Abständen voneinander und entlang zweier auf einen gemeinsamen Punkt zulaufenden Geraden gepflanzten Zypressen eine Tiefenwirkung. Letztere wird verstärkt durch das leicht ansteigende Gelände sowie durch einen dunklen Hintergrund, eine Gruppe imposanter Blutbuchen. Aus der anderen Richtung blickend präsentiert sich ein entgegengesetztes Bild, ohne Tiefenwirkung. Die Baumreihen scheinen von diesem Standpunkt aus betrachtet den Hang hinab parallel zu verlaufen. Die Wirkung, die das Fehlen eines Fluchtpunktes in dieser offenen Ansicht erzeugt, wird durch die Präsenz einer großen isoliert stehenden Konifere verstärkt. Die Zypresse, Cupressus sempervirens, eine der wichtigsten Arten, die seit der Antike kultiviert werden, ist ein Symbol für die Flamme, weibliche Schönheit, Tod, aber auch für die Langlebigkeit: Es wird behauptet, dass tausendjährige Exemplare existieren.

Das Vergnügen, die Ablenkung. Ein »ludischer Wald« (»bosco ludico«) aus Hunderten von Hainbuchen erscheint als eine Insel im bestehenden Gehölzbestand. Mit zunehmendem Wachstum ermöglicht das Wäldchen ein Spiel mit Perspektiven und Blickachsen und wird zum Garten, in dem ein Versteckspiel möglich ist. Geradlinige Wege werden schließlich in einem dichten Wald verlaufen. Dieser Wald ist Teil einer Idee, die ich bereits für einen neuen Stadtpark vorgeschlagen habe. Die Wege sind in einer Weise angelegt, dass der Besucher ständig auf neue Situationen trifft, dass er den einzuschlagenden Weg wählen muss und so neue Entdeckungen machen kann. Die Etymologie des Namens 'Carpinus' von Carpinus betulus ist nicht geklärt. Aber von den möglichen Wortstämmen möchte ich den keltischen zitieren: *car* (Holz) und *pin* (Kopf), der sich auf die Holznutzung für Spiele, auf Spielholz, bezieht. Es handelt sich um kleine Bäume, Reste des Unterholzes großer, uralter Wälder.

Das Erfundene, das Surreale. Eine Reihe in unterschiedliche Richtungen gezogener hoher Sträucher mit pyramidalem Wuchs, Säulen-Hainbuchen, zeichnet eine verdrehte Achse nach, eine »Pflanzenverdrehung« (»torsione vegetale«). Die Sträucher bilden eine Skulptur mit surrealistischem Effekt. Die eng in Reihe gepflanzten Carpinus betulus 'Fastigiata' werden im Laufe der Jahre zu einer vertikalen Wand verwachsen, an der man nur unten eine Drehung wahrnehmen wird, eine Drehung um die jeweils eigene Achse. Diese wird vielleicht selbst für die aufmerksamsten Beobachter nur sichtbar sein.

Das Baumhaus. Linden schaffen einen kleinen kegelförmigen Raum, ein »Lindenhaus« (»casa del tiglio«), ein Spielraum mit einem Fenster

row, the Carpinus betulus 'Fastigiata' shrubs will grow over the course of the years into a tall wall twisted around its own axis, although this effect will only be visible at the bottom. Even then, it is possible that even only the most attentive of observers will notice this aspect.

The tree house. In this folly, linden trees form a small cone-shaped space, a "linden house", a playroom with a window to the sky, a place for children to play. The individual trees will soon grow into a single one, and will one day resemble an old hollow tree. Visitors will tread into it through an opening in its side to look at the trunk from the inside and gaze up at the sky above, visible through the circle formed by the encircling crowns. The linden tree, Tilia, is one of Italy's favourite trees. They can live for over a thousand years and are mentioned in sagas and folk songs. Our ancestors regarded them as sacred, and the experienced and honoured members of communities were given to holding council beneath the old village linden tree.

The follies in this park were created with the wish to use trees and shrubs as the sole means of entertaining and diverting visitors and calling forth amazement, and at the same time to ensure that they form a relationship with existing trees and the special features of the site.

The factor of time is the concept on which the project is based insofar that the playful character of the park as a whole will not become apparent or perceptible until a few decades have passed. Recalling the past is not only an element of re-discovering such aspects of garden design as surprise, playfulness and diversion, but is also entailed in the search for the essential. To quote Sant'Agostino: "Beauty is truth's reflection."

zum Himmel, ein Erlebnisraum für Kinder. Bald werden die einzelnen Linden zu einem einzigen Baum werden, der eines Tages einem alten Baumstamm ähneln wird, in den wir durch einen seitlichen Spalt eintreten werden, um ihn dann von innen zu betrachten und den Himmel durch ein Fenster über uns zu bewundern. Die Linde, Tilia, ist einer unserer Lieblingsbäume. Sie kann über tausend Jahre alt werden und taucht in Sagen und Volksliedern auf. Sie war unseren Vorfahren heilig. Unter der alten Dorflinde berieten einst die Erfahrenen und Ehrwürdigen die Schicksale der Gemeinde.

Die Folies in diesem Park sind aus dem Wunsch entstanden, einzig und allein mit dem Baum als Werkstoff zu belustigen, zu überraschen, Verwunderung zu erzeugen, zu »bauen und zu vermitteln« und dabei gleichzeitig mit den anderen, vor Ort bereits vorhandenen Bäumen und den Besonderheiten des Geländes eine Beziehung aufzubauen. In diesem Projekt formt der Faktor Zeit die Idee. Der spielerische Charakter der Idee wird in seiner Gesamtheit erst nach ein paar Jahrzehnten erleb- und wahrnehmbar werden. Die Erinnerung an die Vergangenheit ist nicht nur bei der Wiederentdeckung der Überraschung, des Spiels und des Vergnügens präsent, sondern auch bei der Suche nach dem Wesentlichen, so wie es Sant' Agostino geschrieben hat: »Schönheit ist der Abglanz des Wahren.«

Die Stammfüße der Säulen-Hainbuchen sind leicht verdreht, die Pflanzenreihe scheint sich um ihre eigene Achse zu drehen (Seite 42 oben). Der »bosco ludico« steht als dichtes Wäldchen in der Wiese und lädt zum Versteckspiel ein (Seite 42 unten). Das Lindenhaus besitzt ein Fenster zum Himmel, die einzelnen Pflanzen wachsen zu einem großen Baum zusammen.

The trunks of the fastigiate hornbeams are slightly twisted at the bottom, with the result that the row of trees seems to twist around its own axis (top opposite). The "bosco ludico" forms a small grove on the meadow, presenting an ideal place for hide-and-seek (bottom opposite). The "linden house" has a window looking up into the sky, and will one day grow into a mighty tree.

Vogelbeobachtungsstationen im Naturpark Kis-Balaton

Bird observation hides at Kis-Balaton Nature Park

Barbara Wiskemann

Das Gebiet um den Kis-Balaton, den kleinen Plattensee, ist Teil des international geschützten Nationalparks Balaton-Oberland. Das Feuchtgebiet beherbergt seltene Tier- und Pflanzenarten und ist vor allem wegen seiner reichen Vogelwelt berühmt: Rund 250 verschiedene Arten können hier beobachtet werden. Auch aus touristischer Sicht ist der Nationalpark ein wichtiger Ort, wird er doch jährlich von vielen naturinteressierten Besuchern aufgesucht. Für diese Besucher an ausgewählten Standorten Vogelbeobachtungsstationen zu entwickeln, setzte sich eine Gruppe von Architekturstudierenden der ETH Zürich zum Ziel. Im Mai sollen sie nun in Ungarn drei der entstandenen Entwürfe selber bauen.

Vögel haben Fluchtdistanzen von 50 bis 100 Metern. Vogelbeobachtungsstationen erlauben den Besuchern, sich den Vögeln unbemerkt bis auf 20 Meter zu nähern.

Diese Kleinbauten sind schlicht: Außer dem Schutz vor Regen bieten sie den Besuchern wenig Komfort und sollen eine Lebensdauer von 10 bis 15 Jahren ohne viel Wartung überstehen. Der Innenraum hat vor allem dunkel zu sein: Ein Schlitz von etwa 25 Zentimetern Höhe gibt die Sicht auf die Umgebung frei, wobei sich die Läden dieser Schlitze nicht nach außen öffnen dürfen: Ein Aufklappen der Läden würde die Tiere für mindestens zwei Stunden verscheuchen. Desgleichen dürfen von außen keine Silhouetten wahrgenommen werden, was bedeutet, dass die Zugänge als einfache Schleusen ausgeführt werden müssen.

Gesucht wurden individuelle Lösungen, bei denen die Beziehung zwischen dem Objekt, dessen Zugang und der Landschaft geklärt wird. Die Konstruktion hat einfach und robust zu sein und soll wenig Unterhaltskosten verursachen. Die Verwendung vor Ort vorhandener

The area around the Kis-Balaton marshlands in Hungary is part of the internationally protected Balaton Uplands National Park. The area is home to rare animal and plant species and is mainly famous for its rich bird life, as indicated by the fact that bird lovers can observe up to 250 species in the park. The national park is also an important place from a tourism point of view, as it is visited every year by numerous nature lovers. It was for these visitors that architecture students at the Swiss Federal Institute of Technology in Zurich (ETH) set themselves the goal of designing bird observation hides. Three of the designs are to be built this year in the marshlands.

Birds usually fly away when people get closer to them than 50 to 100 metres, whereas bird observation hides make it possible to get as close to them as 20 metres. The small structures are generally simple, and apart from providing protection from rain offer little in the way of creature comforts. They should be capable to lasting for 15 to 20 years without requiring many repairs. The interiors have to be dark, and thus feature slits about 25 centimetres high to make it possible to scan the surroundings. Care must be taken to ensure that the shutters on these slits do not open to the outside since this would scare away the birds. It is also important to ensure that silhouettes are not visible from the outside. This means that the hides need to be provided with simple entrance porches.

In other words, solutions that clearly demonstrate the relationship between the object, the entrance porch and the landscape were what was needed. As the designs had to be simple and robust and not require much in the way of maintenance, use of building materials existing at the site suggested itself. Naturally, a task that is so dependent

In einem Naturschutzgebiet am Plattensee werden in diesem Jahr drei individuelle Vogelbeobachtungsstationen gebaut.

Three individual bird observation hides are being built this year at the Hungarian nature reserve on the shore of Lake Balaton.

Für den Entwurf der Vogelbeobachtungsstationen konnten die Studierenden zwischen drei Standorten wählen: ein am Zalakanal liegender Steg (1), ein kleiner, flacher Teich (2) und eine Lösswand in der Nähe der Mündung in den großen Plattensee (3).

In designing the bird observation hides, the students were able to choose between three different locations: a catwalk at the edge of Zala canal (1), a small shallow pond (2), and a loess bluff close to the place where the canal enters Lake Balaton (3).

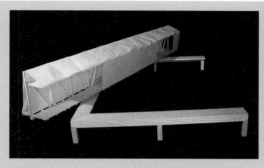

Fachwerkträger: Auf dem vorhandenen Steg wird ein Fachwerkträger aus Holz mit einer Länge von 20,5 und einer Höhe von 2,5 Metern an zwei Punkten schräg aufgelagert. Die auskragenden Enden des Trägers gewährleisten den Sichtschutz für die Zugänge. Um den Träger sind mit Sehschlitzen oder Gucklöchern versehene Stoffbahnen gewickelt, die verschiedene trapezförmige Schnittlösungen zulassen und so den Baukörper in verschiedene Segmente gliedern.
(Entwurf: Andri Gartmann und Nicola Stäubli)

Lattice girder: A wooden lattice girder measuring 20.5 metres in length and 2.5 metres in height will be laid across the landing stage at an angle, resting on it at two points. The cantilevered ends of the girder are to conceal the entrances to the hide from bird life on the lake. Fabric provided with peepholes will be wrapped around some of the filigree braces to form differing spatial segments.
(Design: Andri Gartmann and Nicola Stäubli)

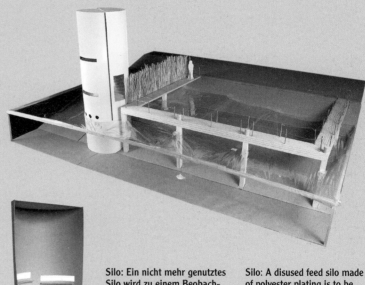

Silo: Ein nicht mehr genutztes Silo wird zu einem Beobachtungsposten umfunktioniert. Um das Silo an der einen Ecke des Steges senkrecht im Kanal aufstellen zu können, wird für die Fundierung der unterste Teil des Silos mit Sand oder Beton ausgegossen. Eine Wendeltreppe im Innern verbindet die drei eingezogenen Böden, Sehschlitze auf verschiedenen Höhen ermöglichen das Herausschauen, Schilfmatten entlang des Steges schirmen den Zugang ab.
(Entwurf: Matthias Uhr und Daniela Heyland)

Silo: A disused feed silo made of polyester plating is to be converted for use as a observation hide at one of the corners of the catwalk. This will involve setting the container into the canal in an upright position, and filling the bottom with sand or concrete. Three floors are to be inserted, and will be connected by a spiral staircase. Slits let into the walls at various heights enable observation of birds, and reed mats conceal the entranceway along the catwalk.
(Design: Matthias Uhr and Daniela Heyland)

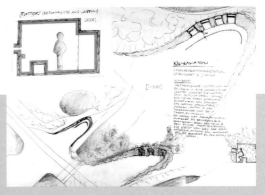

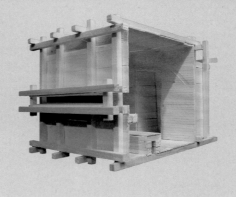

Hecke: Eine geschwungene Hecke mit einer Breite bis zu 2,5 Metern grenzt entlang eines Teiches den Zugang für die Besucher ein. Drei identische Holzgerüste werden in die Hecke eingelassen und in verschiedenen Winkeln auf den Teich ausgerichtet. Sie bieten Besuchern Schutz und lassen den Blick auf Teich und Ufer frei. Die Zugänge, die Sehschlitze und eine Sitzbank sind ebenso wie das Dach der Box mit Brettern verschalt, die Seitenwände sind offen und werden vom Buschwerk verdeckt.
(Entwurf: Sabrina Gehrig und Martin Isch)

Hedge: Three identical wooden hides are to be integrated into an existing hedge at the pond. Aligned to the pond at different angles, the hides will conceal bird watchers and provide a clear view of the pond and its banks. Access to the entrances is provided from behind the hedge, thus hiding approaching visitors, and the open side walls will be covered by the bushes in the hedge. The benches, roofs and details of the entrances and observation slits are made up of boards.
(Design: Sabrina Gehrig and Martin Isch)

Baustoffe ergibt wirtschaftliche und ökologische Vorteile. Und natürlich ist eine solche Bauaufgabe, die derart stark von der Umgebung abhängt und bei der naturbelassene Materialien eine wichtige Rolle spielen, auch ein willkommener Anlass, sich mit der örtlichen Baukultur auseinanderzusetzen.

Doch keine traditionelle Bauten waren gefragt, sondern an die spezifischen Bedingungen angepasste, eigenständige Bauwerke. Diese Voraussetzungen führten in einigen Fällen zur Wiederaufnahme archaischer Bauweisen: Techniken wie das Schichten, Stecken, Flechten, Graben oder Wickeln wurden zu zentralen Themen der Entwürfe.

on the surroundings and that involves use of untreated natural materials requires preoccupation with local construction means. However, the challenge was not to reproduce traditional buildings but create structures that take specific conditions into consideration while demonstrating a character of their own. This led to the use of archaic building means, with the result that methods involving layering, weaving, digging and wrapping are the central themes of the designs.

Bird observation hides at Kis-Balaton Nature Park
Client: Balaton Uplands National Park, Kis-Balaton District Board for Water Systems
Planning and execution: Balaton Team, Swiss Federal Institute of Technology,
Zurich: Prof. Andrea Deplazes (architecture and structural design), Prof. Dr. Ákos
Moravánszky (theory of architecture), Prof. Dr. Otto Künzle (load-bearing
structures), and various students and assistants
Planning: November 2002 – May 2003
Construction: May 2003

Der Architekt als Korbmacher

The architect as a basket weaver

Until today there has been no significant building in Europe constructed by a Japanese architect. Despite all the assertions of ties and reference to the formal similarity between the Early Modern in the West and traditional architecture in the Far East, the discussions about questions of space never went beyond the dimension of exhibition contributions and pavilions. The small contributions at world exhibitions and festivals were often heavily weighed down by the symbolism attached to them and were pulled down again at the end of the event.

The Japanese architect Toyo Ito presented two pavilions in Europe in the summer of 2002 in a considerably more liberated fashion. A small construction in each case, on the central square in Bruges and in front of the Serpentine Gallery in Hyde Park in London present the space they create and the environment they reflect as a focus. Both the pavilions show clearly – as seldom before – the different interpretations of space in European and Japanese architecture. Whereas in the Germanic language the term "space" derives from the idea of a clearing, i.e. by clearing a free space in a densely wooded region, the Japanese word for space, *kukan*, is made up of the characters for air and interval. The understanding to be interpreted from this of "space as a field in infinity" stands diametrically to the idea of "space as a clearing". Following the European interpretation, space can be understood as a vessel, the Japanese interpretation as a basket. In Bruges and London, Toyo Ito placed a basket in the vessel of the European urban area.

The tension between these two principles of space formation runs through Toyo Ito's entire work. If one traces his work back to the begin-

Bis heute gibt es in Europa kein bedeutendes Bauwerk eines japanischen Architekten. Trotz aller Beteuerungen von Verbundenheit und dem Verweis auf die formale Ähnlichkeit zwischen früher Moderne im Westen und traditioneller Baukunst in Fernost ging der Austausch bezüglich Fragen des Raumes über die Dimension von Ausstellungsbeiträgen und Pavillons nie hinaus. Die kleinen Beiträge bei Weltausstellungen und Festivals trugen oft schwer an der ihnen aufgebürdeten Symbolik und wurden nach Ende des Spektakels wieder abgerissen.

Wesentlich befreiter präsentierte der japanische Architekt Toyo Ito im Sommer 2002 zwei Pavillons in Europa: Je ein kleiner Bau auf dem zentralen Platz in Brügge und vor der Serpentine Gallery im Hyde Park in London stellen nichts anderes als den Raum, den sie schaffen, und die Umgebung, die sie widerspiegeln, in den Mittelpunkt. Die beiden Pavillons zeigen so deutlich wie selten zuvor die unterschiedliche Raumauffassung zwischen europäischer und japanischer Baukultur. Während sich in den germanischen Sprachen der Begriff Raum aus dem Wort Rodung, also dem Herausschneiden eines Leerraums aus einer dichten Umgebung ableitet, so ist das japanische Wort für Raum, *kukan*, aus den Zeichen für Luft und Intervall zusammengesetzt. Das daraus zu interpretierende Verständnis von »Raum als einem Feld im Unendlichen« steht der Idee von »Raum als Rodung« diametral entgegen. Der europäischen Auffassung folgend kann Raum als Gefäß verstanden werden, der japanischen Interpretation nach als Korb. Toyo Ito setzte in Brügge und in London in das Gefäß des europäischen Stadtraums einen Korb.

Die Spannung zwischen diesen beiden Prinzipien der Raumbildung zieht sich durch Toyo Itos Gesamtwerk. Verfolgt man sein Werk zu den Anfängen zurück, so fächert sich sein Œuvre auf: Ein frühes Meisterwerk war ein Gefäß – das »White U« in Tokyo aus dem Jahr 1976, ein hermetisch abgeschlossenes Haus ohne Fenster. Bisheriger Höhepunkt ist ein Korb – die Mediathek in Sendai, Japan, aus dem Jahr 2000, ein vollkommen transparentes Gebäude ohne Wände. Diese Entwicklung vom Haus als »Keil gegen das Chaos der Stadt« zum Gebäude als »Verwirbelung im urbanen Fluss« dokumentiert, dass der Architekt unsere Lebensumwelt als einen Gesamtraum versteht. Schon 1988 äußerte Ito

Nikolaus Knebel

Im Sommer 2002 baute Toyo Ito in Brügge und in London je einen Pavillon mit fließenden Grenzen zwischen Innen und Außen.

In 2002, Toyo Ito built two pavilions, one in Bruges and one in London, with a merging transition from the interior to the exterior.

diese als Schlüssel zu seinem Werk dienende Auffassung: »Anders als die Städte in Europa, haben unsere Städte (in Japan) kein Außen, und daher haben wir auch im Stadtraum nicht den Eindruck, draußen zu sein. (...) Ein Raum, bei dem man immer das Gefühl hat, drinnen zu sein – das ist für mich der Idealzustand einer Architektur.«

In dem selben Essay verweist Ito auf das Motiv der Urhütte, mit dem der französische Architekturtheoretiker Marc-Antoine Laugier im 18. Jahrhundert den Ursprung der Architektur herleitete. Die Geschichte der Suche nach einer Behausung beschreibt Laugier mit dem Niederlassen des Menschen an einem Fluss. An diesem Ort ist der Mensch eins mit der Natur. Doch um sich vor Regen und Sonne zu schützen, flüchtet er in eine Höhle. Wegen der unbehaglichen Dunkelheit und Feuchtigkeit verlässt er sie aber, kehrt schließlich wieder zum Fluss zurück und baut dort eine Hütte. Diese Urhütte steht zwischen vier Bäumen, deren Äste und Zweige miteinander verflochten werden. Der so entstehende Bau ist integraler Bestandteil der Natur. Diesen Gedanken nimmt Toyo Ito auf und erweitert ihn um das Verständnis der heutigen Stadt als zweite Natur. Auch in einer künstlichen Umwelt, die analog zu den Luft- und Wasserströmen der natürlichen Umgebung von elektronischen und infrastrukturellen Flüssen gekennzeichnet ist, bleibt das Ideal einer in die – zweite – Natur integrier-

ning, his oeuvre unfolds thus: An early masterpiece was a vessel – the "White U" in Tokyo from the year 1976, a hermetically enclosed house without windows. The highlight until now is a basket – the Mediathek in Sendai, Japan, from the year 2000, a completely transparent building without walls. This development from a house as a "wedge in the urban chaos" to the building as a "whirl in the urban river" documents that the architect understands our life environment as one entire space. In 1988 Ito already expressed this interpretation serving as the key to his work: "Unlike the towns in Europe our towns (in Japan) have no exterior and therefore we do not have the impression of being outside, within the urban area. (...) A space in which one always has the feeling of being inside – for me that is the ideal state for architecture."

In the same essay Ito makes reference to the motif of the primeval hut, from which the French architecture-theoretician, Marc-Antoine Laugier derived the origin of architecture in the 18th century. Laugier explains the history of the search for shelter with settlements along a river. At this place the human is one with nature. But to protect himself from the rain and sun he withdraws inside a cave. Due to the uncomfortable darkness and damp however, he leaves it and finally returns to the river and builds a hut there. This primeval hut stands between four trees, with interwoven branches and twigs. The construction thus formed is an integral part of nature. Toyo Ito takes up this thought and extends it to the understanding of today's town as second nature. Also in an artificial environment, which, analogous to the currents of air and water in the natural environment, is char-

acterised by electronic and infrastructural currents, the ideal remains of an architecture integrated into – second – nature. "For us, the town dwellers, it is important", writes Ito, "to visualise the primeval shelter once again. For in the forest of the urban area, a river can be the flow of traffic on an autobahn, or even the invisible flow of electromagnetic waves, and the cool shadow under a tree might only be found in a forest of steel and aluminium struts (...). Our primeval hut, created for us to dwell in, resembles a kind of shelter that is only enveloped by a soft, invisible veil, but contrary to Laugier, is without a clear structure of supports, beams and roofing timber-work." The architectural plan for the pavilion erected fifteen years later is already being suggested here.

ten Architektur bestehen. »Für uns, die Stadtbewohner, ist es bedeutsam«, schreibt Ito, »uns die Urhütte noch einmal zu vergegenwärtigen. Denn im Wald des Stadtraums, mag ein Fluss der Verkehrsfluss einer Autobahn, oder sogar der unsichtbare Strom elektromagnetischer Wellen sein, und der kühle Schatten unter einem Baum mag nur in einem Wald von Stahl- und Aluminium-Balken (...) zu finden sein. Unsere Urhütte, geschaffen, um uns zu behausen, wird so etwas wie ein Unterstand sein, der nur von einem weichen, unsichtbaren Schleier umhüllt ist, aber anders als bei Laugier eine klare Struktur aus Stütze, Träger und Dachgebälk vermissen lässt.« Der Bauplan für die fünfzehn Jahre später errichteten Pavillons klingt hier schon an.

Die Pavillons stellen den aktuellsten Versuch dar, eine Urhütte zu bauen. Beide Räume haben, so Ito, »Qualitäten, die näher an denen der Natur als der Architektur sind. Vielleicht ist dies der Anfang einer freien Beziehung zwischen der natürlichen Umgebung und dem menschlichen Tun.« Sowohl in Brügge, als auch in London reduzieren die als Ein-Raum konzipierten Pavillons das Augenmerk auf die Hülle, die – wie der oben beschriebene Schleier – zugleich tragend und transparent sein soll. Folglich

The pavilions represent the most modern attempt at building a primeval hut. Both spaces have, so Ito, "qualities that are closer to nature than the architecture. Perhaps this is the beginning of a liberated relationship between the natural environment and the human's doing." Both in Bruges and in London the pavilions conceived as a single room reduce the attention to the envelopment that – like the above-mentioned veil – is to be a bearing structure and transparent at the same time. As a consequence, no differentiation is made any longer between primary and secondary structure or between skin and bones. On the contrary, the supports, roof and façade merge to form a single web that lends the pavilions the sense of unity of a massive construction and the transparency of a light-weight one. Despite the same intention, namely of marking a place in the environment understood as one entire space as reservedly as possible, the envelopments of both constructions are produced differently.

Yet whether the envelopment as in Bruges is produced according to the principle of weaving or as in London, the principle of felting, the central motif remains as the merging of the boundary between the interior and exterior. This "blurring architecture", as Ito calls his work, is the opposite of "the inside being different to the outside", which still characterises the architecture in the European towns. Ito has made a considerable contribution towards this dispute between the architect as a vessel-maker and the architect as a basket-weaver. The fact that both pavilions have already been taken down again is all the more regrettable if one considers that to this very day, there has been no significant building in Europe constructed by a Japanese architect.

Anlässlich der Ernennung Brügges zur Europäischen Kulturhauptstadt 2002 baute Toyo Ito auf einem zentralen Platz in der Altstadt einen temporären Pavillon. Die Aluminiumkonstruktion öffnete sich an den Stirnseiten zur Stadt.

On the occasion of Bruges' designation as the European Cultural Capital 2002, Toyo Ito built a temporary pavilion on a central square in the old part of the town. The front of the aluminium structure opens up to the city.

wird nicht mehr zwischen Primär- und Sekundärstruktur oder zwischen Haut und Knochen unterschieden. Vielmehr verschmelzen Stütze, Decke und Fassade zu einem einzigen Gewebe, das den Pavillons die Einheit eines Massivbaus und die Transparenz eines Leichtbaus verleiht. Trotz gleicher Intention, nämlich einen Ort in der als Gesamtraum begriffenen Umwelt möglichst zurückhaltend zu markieren, sind die Hüllen bei beiden Bauten unterschiedlich gefertigt.

Doch ob die Hülle wie in Brügge nach dem Prinzip des Verwebens, oder wie in London nach dem Prinzip des Verfilzens gemacht ist, das zentrale Motiv bleibt das Verschwimmen der Grenze zwischen Innen und Außen. Dieses »blurring architecture«, wie Ito sein Werk überschreibt, ist das Gegenteil jenes »drinnen-ist-anders-als-draußen«, das die Architektur der europäischen Stadt nach wie vor prägt. Zu dieser Auseinandersetzung zwischen dem Architekten als Gefäßmacher und dem Architekten als Korbmacher hat Toyo Ito einen bedeutenden Beitrag geleistet. Dass die beiden Pavillons schon wieder abgebaut worden sind, ist bedauerlich, da es somit in Europa immer noch kein bedeutendes Bauwerk eines japanischen Architekten gibt.

In der Fassade des Brügger Pavillons wechselten filigrane Wabenmuster mit ovalen Aluminiumplatten. Das Gitter verlieh dem Bau Transparenz und Leichtigkeit, die Paneele gaben ihm die notwendige Stabilität.

Filigreed honeycombs alternate with oval aluminium plates in the façade of the Bruges pavilion. The grid lent the construction a sense of transparency and lightness, the panels provided the necessary stability.

Parasitäre Architekturen

Parasitic architecture

Anneke Bokern

Kleine Bauten auf bestehenden Gebäuden zapfen wie Parasiten ihren Wirt an, verhelfen ihnen aber auch zu neuem Leben.

Small structures on existing buildings live off their hosts like parasites, but also providing them with new life energy.

Parasiten sind im Allgemeinen keine sonderlich beliebten Zeitgenossen. Die Biologie definiert sie als Bakterien-, Pflanzen- oder Tierarten, die ihre Nahrung anderen Lebewesen entnehmen. Man unterscheidet zwischen temporären Parasiten, die sich nur vorübergehend im Körper ihres Wirtes aufhalten, und stationären Parasiten, die es sich dort dauerhaft gemütlich machen. Es gibt Parasiten, die nur unter bestimmten Bedingungen schmarotzen (fakultative Parasiten), und solche, die gar nicht anders können (obligate Parasiten). Manche der Kreaturen, genannt Ektoparasiten, lassen sich auf der Körperoberfläche ihres Wirtes nieder, während andere, die sogenannten Endoparasiten, in sein Inneres eindringen.

Gemeinsam ist ihnen allen ihr schlechter Ruf. Ob Fuchsbandwurm oder Holzbock, Leberegel oder Fadenwurm – hinterhältig sind sie, hartnäckig und ekelhaft. Gleichzeitig beeindrucken Parasiten durch ihre subtilen, unglaublich erfolgreichen Überlebensstrategien. Ein prekäres Gleichgewicht kennzeichnet jegliches parasitäre Verhältnis: Der Parasit zapft dem Wirt Energie ab, darf diesen aber nicht töten, solange er auf ihn angewiesen ist. Nützliche Parasiten kann es per Definition nicht geben, denn ziehen beide Seiten Nutzen aus dem Verhältnis, so handelt es sich nicht mehr um Parasitismus, sondern um eine Symbiose. Allein der Mensch hat gelernt, sich manche Parasiten zunutze zu machen – so etwa, wenn er Blutegel zum Aderlass einsetzt oder mit Hilfe von Parasiten biologische Schädlingsbekämpfung betreibt.

Aber auch das konnte die Reputation der Tierchen nicht retten. Dabei war es ursprünglich gar nicht ehrenrührig, als Parasit bezeichnet zu werden. Ein »parasitos«, wörtlich übersetzt ein »Mitesser«, war im antiken Griechenland ein hochangesehener Opferbeamter, der an rituellen Gastmählern für die Götter teilnehmen durfte. Allerdings erfuhr der Begriff noch in der Antike eine negative Umdeutung und bezeichnete seither vor allem einen Menschen, der auf Kosten anderer lebt, bis er um 1825 seinen Weg in die naturwissenschaftlichen Lexika fand.

Parasitismus bleibt nie ohne Folgen, stets verursacht der Eindringling eine Veränderung im Wirt, sei sie erwünscht oder unerwünscht. Manch ein Parasit in der Natur polt seinen Wirt um und lässt ihn plötzlich Dinge tun, die ihm völlig wesensfremd sind.

Parasites are not generally considered to be all that popular. Biology defines them as species of bacteria, plants or animals that live in or on another organism. A differentiation is made between parasites that only live temporarily in the organism of their host and stationary parasites that make themselves comfortable there permanently. There are parasites that only exploit other organisms under certain conditions (facultative parasites), and others that cannot do otherwise (obligatory parasites). Some of these creatures, called ectoparasites, live on the outside of their host whereas the others, the so-called endoparasites, penetrate inside it.

What they all have in common is their bad reputation. Whether tapeworms or ticks – they are insidious, obstinate and repulsive. Nevertheless, the subtle, unbelievably successful survival strategies of these parasites are impressive. A precarious balance characterises any parasitic association: The parasite taps energy from its host, but cannot afford to kill it as long as it is dependent on it. However, by definition parasites cannot be useful, for if both sides were to benefit from the association, parasitism would no longer be involved, but a symbiosis. Only humans have learned to make use of some of these parasites – for instance, when a leech is used for phlebotomy or when biological pest control is carried out with the help of parasites.

But not even that could rid these organisms of their bad reputation. Originally it was by no means considered defamatory to be called a parasite. The English word "parasite" was formerly used to describe a person with whom one dined; in Ancient Greece "parasitos" was a highly revered sacrificial officer who was allowed to partake in the feasts for the deities. Nevertheless, the term already took on a negative connotation in classical antiquity; since then it has been mainly applied to a person who exploits others, then finding its way into scientific encyclopaedias around 1825.

Parasitism never remains without consequences; the invader always causes a change in its host, whether this is desired, or not. Many a parasite in nature reverses the behaviour of its host, thereby suddenly causing it to do things that are totally against its nature.

This principle of smaller invaders bringing influence to bear on large organisms is also copied time and again in architecture. An early example of a parasitic building is to be found in Mezquita in Córdoba. After the Spaniards had reconquered the town, they planted a chapel in Renaissance style in the middle of the column setting of the Arabian mosque – an endoparasite that, despite it having an aesthetically disturbing effect, enabled the mosque that had become useless after the reconquista to be preserved. The parasite was able to breathe new life into the building by changing its character.

Over the past few years, the Parasite Foundation Rotterdam has set itself the task of planting similar parasites strategically on buildings or in an urban setting. The initiative taken by the architects' office Korteknie & Stuhlmacher uses parasitic buildings for brightening up dilapidated host buildings or locations. The parasites nest temporarily in discovered niches and help themselves to the infrastructure of their host; however, contrary to their namesakes in nature, they do not suck out any vital juices but provide the organism with energy. In this connection the word "parasite" has several meanings: On the one had it stands for "Prototypes for Advanced Ready-made Amphibious Small-scale Individual Temporary Ecological houses", and on the other, for "para-

Dieses Prinzip der Einflussnahme kleiner Eindringlinge auf große Organismen nimmt sich auch die Architektur immer wieder einmal zum Vorbild. Ein frühes Beispiel für einen parasitären Bau findet sich in der Mezquita in Córdoba. Nach der Rückeroberung der Stadt von den Mauren pflanzten die Spanier in die Mitte der Säulenlandschaft der arabischen Moschee eine Kapelle im Renaissance-Stil – ein Endoparasit, der zwar ästhetisch störend wirkt, aber ermöglichte, dass die nach der Reconquista eigentlich nutzlos gewordene Moschee erhalten blieb. Der Parasit konnte dem Bau durch eine Veränderung seines Wesens neues Leben einhauchen.

Eine ähnlich strategische Platzierung von Parasiten an Gebäuden oder im Stadtzusammenhang hat sich in den letzten Jahren die Parasite Foundation Rotterdam zur Aufgabe gemacht. Die Initiative des Architekturbüros Korteknie & Stuhlmacher setzt parasitäre Gebäude ein, um kränkelnde Wirtsbauten oder -orte wiederzubeleben. Die Parasiten nisten sich zeitweise in vorgefundene Nischen ein, bedienen sich der Infrastruktur des Wirts, saugen jedoch im Gegenteil zu ihren Namensvettern in der Natur keinen Lebenssaft ab, sondern versorgen den Organismus mit Energie.

In diesem Zusammenhang hat das Wort »Parasite« mehrere Bedeutungen: Einerseits steht es für »Prototypes for Advanced Ready-made Amphibious Small-scale Individual Temporary Ecological houses«, andererseits für

Der kleine Holzbau auf einer Abstandsgrünfläche des Rotterdamer Vorortes Hoogvliet beherbergt ein Nachbarschaftszentrum. Das Gebäude soll dazu beitragen, dem heruntergekommenen Stadtteil neues Leben einzuhauchen. (Architekten: Marcel Meili, Markus Peter Architekten, Zürich; Holzbau: Schilliger Holz AG und Blumer-Lehmann AG)

The small wooden building on a green buffer space of Rotterdam's satellite town Hoogvliet accommodates a so-called neighbourhood centre. The building should help breathing new life into the dilapidated city district. (Architects: Marcel Meili, Markus Peter Architects, Zurich; wood construction: Schilliger Holz AG, Blumer Lehmann AG)

Auf dem Liftschacht eines ehemaligen Werkstattbaus in Rotterdam befindet sich der erste von Korteknie & Stuhlmacher realisierte Parasit. Er entstand im Rahmen des Kulturhauptstadtprogrammes Rotterdam im Sommer 2001. Der kleine giftgrüne Aufbau beherbergt ein zweigeschossiges Modellhaus. Die großen Fensteröffnungen lassen den Blick frei auf die vielfältige Stadtlandschaft der Umgebung.

The first parasite which Korteknie & Stuhlmacher were able to construct sits on the lift shaft of a former factory building in Rotterdam. It originated within the framework of the Rotterdam Cultural Capital program in summer of 2001. The small, garish green construction accommodates a 2-storey model house. The spacious window openings provide a view of the diverse urban landscape of the surrounding area.

»Para-Sites«, also verlassene Randstandorte, deren temporäre Nutzung zur experimentellen Stadtverdichtung beitragen kann. Die Parasiten sollen das Potential von Orten erkunden, die als unbewohnbar gelten, sie für begrenzte Zeit in den Stadtzusammenhang zurückführen und so auf mögliche zukünftige Nutzungen verweisen.

Der erste Parasit, den Korteknie & Stuhlmacher realisieren konnten, sitzt auf dem Dach eines ehemaligen Werkstattbaus in Rotterdam. Klein, giftgrün und weithin sichtbar hockt »LP2« auf dem Liftschacht des riesigen »Las Palmas«-Gebäudes auf der Hafenhalbinsel Kop van Zuid. Ähnlich dem namensgebenden Ungeziefer, zapft der Parasit die Infrastruktur seines Wirtsbaus an: Wasser- und Stromleitungen des Modell-Wohnhauses hängen am System des Las Palmas, das von der Stadt Rotterdam zeitweise als Kulturzentrum und Ausstellungsgebäude genutzt wird.

Im Kontext der Stadtlandschaft bewirkt der Parasit einen visuellen Juckreiz. Trotz oder gerade wegen seiner geringen Größe zieht er zwischen

sites", for example deserted places in the outskirts, the temporary utilisation of which is able to contribute towards experimental urban concentration. The parasites have the task of seeking potential in places that are deemed as uninhabitable, to win them back into the town context and thereby draw attention to possible future utilisation.

The first parasite which Korteknie & Stuhlmacher were able to construct sits on the roof of a former factory building in Rotterdam. The "LP 2", crouching on the lift shaft of the enormous "Las Palmas" building on the peninsular port of Kop van Zuid, is small, of a poisonous green and visible from a long distance away. Similar to the vermin after which it is named, the parasite taps the infrastructure of its host's building. The water-

Der Aufbau mit dem Namen LP2 zapft wie ein richtiger Parasit die Infrastruktur seines Wirtes an und bezieht von ihm Wasser und Strom. Das Gebäude aus Massivholz-Platten kann in seine Einzelteile zerlegt und an einem neuen Ort wieder aufgebaut werden. Ziel der »Parasite Foundation Rotterdam« ist es, über das ganze Land verstreut ihre mobilen Gebäude anzusiedeln.

The construction, named LP2, taps the infrastructure of its host just like a real parasite – drawing water and energy from it. The building made from solid wood plates can be broken down into its component parts and re-erected elsewhere. The "Parasite Foundation Rotterdam" has set itself the task of spreading their mobile buildings all over the country.

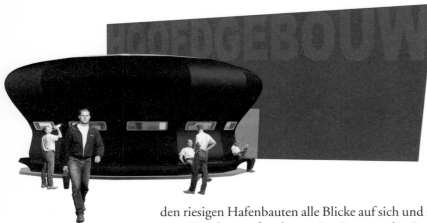

den riesigen Hafenbauten alle Blicke auf sich und macht damit auch auf seinen Wirtsbau aufmerksam. Im Inneren des Parasiten lenken strategisch platzierte Fenster den Blick auf die Stadtlandschaft. So gibt eine offene Ecke im ersten Stockwerk einen panoramahaften Blick über die Lagerhausdächer des Kop van Zuid frei, während ein großes Fenster im zweiten Stock den Blick nach Südosten, in Richtung des Wilhelminaplein lenkt. Einige kleinere Fenster sind an völlig unerwarteten Stellen, teils sogar auf Fußbodenniveau eingelassen und gewähren selektive Ausblicke auf den Fluss, vorbeiziehende Schiffe und die umstehenden Hochhäuser.

Wie der Las-Palmas-Parasit die Hafenlandschaft inszeniert und zeitweise zur Sehenswürdigkeit erhebt, so lenkt auch der zweite realisierte Parasit, ein Entwurf des Schweizer Architekturbüros Meili Peter, die Aufmerksamkeit auf seinen quasi-urbanen Kontext. Seit letztem Frühjahr steht der kleine Holzbau auf einem Stück Abstandsgrün in der Rotterdamer Satellitenstadt Hoogvliet und dient als Nachbarschaftszentrum. Die Rolle des Wirtes spielt hier kein einzelnes Gebäude, sondern die recht heruntergekommene, gesichtslose Schlafstadt Hoogvliet selbst. In den nächsten Jahren sollen in dieser Stadterweiterung, die in den sechziger Jahren für die Arbeiter der nahen Shell-Fabrik errichtet wurde, zahlreiche Siedlungen abgerissen werden. Auch die niedriggeschossigen Seniorenwohnungen, die den Parasiten umgeben, werden der Abrissbirne zum Opfer fallen.

Durch seine eigenständige Form und die Positionierung mitten auf der Grünfläche ist der Parasit ein Hingucker im höhepunktarmen Hoogvliet. Als Nachbarschaftszentrum erfüllt er außerdem eine soziale Funktion, die der todgeweihten Siedlung bisher fehlte und vielleicht sogar einen belebenden Effekt haben kann. Parasitenbefall als Therapie.

In diesem Sinne entwarfen auch Christoph Seyferth, das Architekturbüro ONIX und Barend Koolhaas vom Büro OI drei »SchoolParasites« für die Parasite Foundation. Als unselbständige »Untermieter« sollen die

pipes and electric cables of this model of residential building are connected to the system of Las Palmas that is temporarily used by the town of Rotterdam as a cultural centre and exhibition building.

In the context of the urban setting, the parasite is a visual eye-sore. Despite or even because of its insignificant size, it attracts everyone's attention, set between the enormous port buildings and in this way also draws attention to its host's building. Inside the parasite, strategically positioned windows direct one's view to the urban landscape. In this way, an open corner on the first floor provides a panoramic view of the warehouse roofs of Kop van Zuid, whereas a large window on the second floor directs one's gaze in the direction of the Wilhelminaplein. Several smaller windows are in completely unexpected places and provide selective views of the river, and the surrounding buildings.

Just as the Las Palmas parasite stages the port setting and temporarily exalts it to the rank of a "sight", another parasite – a project designed by the Swiss architects' office Meili Peter, also attracts one's attention to its quasi-urban context. Since last spring, the small wooden building has stood on a small green buffer zone in Rotterdam's satellite town Hoogvliet and serves as a so-called neighbourhood centre. The role of the host is not played here by any one building, but by the decaying, characterless dormitory town of Hoogvliet itself. In the next few years a large number of houses are to be pulled down in this urban colony which were erected in the 60's. Also the somewhat lower residence blocks for the elderly surrounding the parasites are to become victim of the demolition plans.

Due to its individual form and positioning, directly in the centre of the green, the parasite is a focus of attraction in this uneventful town of

Hoogvliet. As a neighbourhood centre, it additionally fulfils a social function that had been lacking until now and perhaps it can even have a reviving effect: Parasitic infestation as a therapy.

To this end, Christoph Seyfert, the architects' office ONIX and Barend Koolhaas at OI also designed three "school parasites" for the Parasite Foundation. As non-independent "sub-tenants", the pavilions are to serve the Hoogvliet primary schools as provisional buildings in their financial straits and provide for lacking social functions.

All these parasites have one thing in common, and that is, they paradoxically bring benefit to the host instead of exploiting it or doing it any damage. Another approach has been made, on the other hand, by the American artist, Michael Rakowitz, with his paraSITES. He designed a series of tent-like dwellings for the homeless that are connected to the exhaust pipes of houses and are blown up and heated by this warm air. His parasites are therefore mobile architectural constructions for people who have no option other than mobility. These parasites, too, purposely create an optical contrast to their host and want to draw attention in this way to the town's homeless, who are often discredited as being the "parasites in our society". The available architecture signifies a body, the respiratory and digestive organs of which produce sufficient surplus energy for the weaker, dependent organisms.

Parasitic building structures are small interventions with a tremendous effect. Contrary to the current strategies in urban planning of demolishing and rebuilding, or completely transforming unutilised places, they first give rise to a purely mental re-assessment of their location. In the optimum case, they thereby reveal architectonic possibilities that have not been discovered until now.

Die Parasiten des amerikanischen Künstlers Michael Rakowitz dienen einem sozialen Zweck: Zeltartige Hüllen aus Kunststoff werden an die Abluftrohre von Häusern angedockt. Die warme Luft bläst die Hüllen auf, die so Obdachlosen als Schlafstätte zur Verfügung stehen.

The parasites by the American artist, Michael Rakowitz, serve a social cause. Tent-like plastic shells are connected to the exhaust pipes of houses. Inflated by the warm air, the shells provide a place to sleep for the homeless.

Pavillons Hoogvlieter Grundschulen in Geldnot als Behelfsbauten dienen und fehlende soziale Funktionen ergänzen.

All diesen Parasiten ist gemeinsam, dass sie dem Wirt paradoxerweise Nutzen bringen, anstatt ihn auszusaugen oder ihm zu schaden. Einen anderen Ansatz verfolgt dagegen der amerikanische Künstler Michael Rakowitz mit seinen paraSITES. Er entwarf eine Reihe zeltartiger Behausungen für Obdachlose, die an die Abluftrohre von Häusern angeschlossen werden können und sich durch die warme Luft aufblasen und erwärmen. Seine Parasiten sind somit mobile Architekturen für Menschen, die keine andere Wahl als die Mobilität haben. Auch diese Parasiten heben sich optisch bewusst von ihrem Wirt ab und wollen so auf die Obdachlosen in der Stadt – oft als »Schmarotzer der Gesellschaft« verschrien – aufmerksam machen. Die vorhandene Architektur wird als Körper gedeutet, dessen Atmungs- und Verdauungsorgane genug überschüssige Energie für schwächere, abhängige Organismen produzieren.

Parasitäre Bauten sind kleine Eingriffe mit großer Wirkung. Im Gegensatz zu den gängigen städtebaulichen Strategien von Abriss und Neubau oder völliger Transformation ungenutzter Orte, bewirken sie zunächst eine rein gedankliche Umbewertung ihres Wohnorts. Im besten Falle öffnen sie damit den Blick für bisher unentdeckte architektonische Möglichkeiten.

Vom Müssen, Dürfen und Machen

Having to go, being able to go – and going

Axel Simon

Die Lage ist beschissen, keine Frage. Deutschland gibt sich bedürfnisfeindlich, und woanders ist es mit dem öffentlichen Stuhlgang selten besser bestellt. Findet der Müssende einen Ort, wo er darf, lautet die Devise meistens: Nase zu und durch – oder er zieht den Gang zu McDonalds oder den Baum im Park vor.

Das Erleichtern in der Öffentlichkeit muss allerdings nicht zwangsläufig Atembeschwerden oder schlechtes Gewissen hervorrufen. Der Blick in die Vergangenheit zeigt: Das Machen kann Spaß machen, so wie das Sitzen in einem Café, das Lesen eines Buches oder Spazierengehen. Das Mekka des öffentlichen Geschäftes ist und bleibt Paris. Walter Benjamin hat das Pissoir als wichtige Einrichtung in der Wohnung des Flaneurs, der Strasse, zwar vergessen zu erwähnen, doch schon in den 1830er Jahren wurden sie in der Hauptstadt des 19. Jahrhunderts installiert – ohne beim Bürgertum Proteststürme auszulösen, wie zum Beispiel in München und Wien einige Jahrzehnte später. Den intimen Bezug, den die Pariser zu ihren öffentlichen Abtritten pflegen, zeigen die fast zärtlichen Namen, die sie ihnen gaben: »Rambuteaus« hießen die allerersten – Reklamesäulen mit eingebautem Pissoir, die der Präfekt gleichen Namens aufstellen ließ. Das etwas enge Modell lösten die »Vespasiennes« ab, reihen- oder sternförmig angeordnete Piss-Stände ohne Dach, umschlossen von einer hüfthohen Eisenwand. Benannt sind sie nach dem römischen Kaiser, der einst gesagt haben soll, Geld stinke nicht, als Erwiderung auf Kritik an der von ihm erhobenen Steuer auf das Urin seiner Untertanen – was wiederum darauf schließen lässt, dass auch die Pariser schon früh etwas berappen mussten. Selbst die unpersönlichsten Aborte bedenken sie mit Kosenamen: Die erstmals 1980 von Jean-Claude Decaux entwickelten Vollautomaten mit eingebauter All-over-Desinfektion, Handwäsche und musikalischer Begleitung nennen sie »Sanisette«.

Müssen in der Stadt macht durchaus Spaß, wenn das Umfeld passt – ein Seitenblick aufs öffentliche Notdurft-Verrichten.

Having "to go" in the town can be good fun if the surroundings are right – a side look at the public convenience in use.

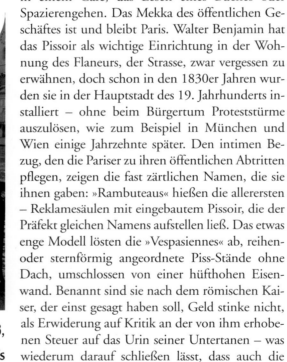

The situation is shitty – there's no doubt about it. Germany takes on a hostile attitude towards this pressing need and the situation for relieving nature in public is seldom any better elsewhere. If the person who has to "go" finds a place to do so then his motto is: Hold your nose tight and "go" – or he gives preference to McDonalds or the tree in the park. Relieving nature in public, however, must not necessarily cause respiratory problems or a bad conscience. A glance in the past shows that "going to the toilet" can be enjoyable, just like sitting in a café, reading a good book in the sun, or going for a walk.

The Mecca for public conveniences is and remains Paris. Walter Benjamin forgot to mention the urinal as an important facility in the stroller's home, in the street, but in the 1830's they were already installed in the capital of the 19th century – without causing storms of protest amongst the population, such as for example in Munich and Vienna some centuries later. The intimate association that the Parisians have with their public conveniences is shown by the quasi affectionate names they gave to them: "Rambuteaus" was the name given to the very first ones, i.e. advertising pillars with an integrated urinal that was named after the administrative officer who had them installed. The "Vespasiennes" gave way to this rather cramped model – urinals set in a row or star-shaped arrangement without a roof and enclosed by a waist-high wrought-iron wall. They were called after the Roman Emperor who is once to have said that money does not stink in retort to criticism about the tax he levied on the urine of his subjects – which in turn implies that the Paris population also had to pay for this very early on. They even give nicknames to the most im-

personal toilets. They call the first fully automatic toilets with integrated all-over disinfection, hand-wash and musical accompaniment developed by Jean-Claude Decaux in 1980, the "Sanisette".

Calvinist Zurich presented its lavatories considerably later than post-revolutionary Paris, but

Zwar wesentlich später als das nach-revolutionäre Paris, aber ähnlich stolz, präsentierte das calvinistische Zürich seine Bedürfnisanstalten. Um 1900 gehörten Pissoirs sogar vor Kirchenportalen zum gewohnten Bild – gleiches war etwa im katholischen Wien undenkbar. Hier gelang es den Behörden erst in den 1930er Jahren eine Einrichtung für die einschlägigen Bedürfnisse der Passanten am Stephansplatz durchzusetzen – und das auch nur unterirdisch und mit einem schamhaften »Hier«-Schild gekennzeich-

net. In Zürich entwarfen die Stadtbaumeister persönlich die Häuschen. Teilweise städtebaulich prominent gelegen, schmücken Füllhörner ihren Eingang, über dem eine Uhr prangt, sonst bedeutenden Gebäuden wie Kirchen oder Bahnhöfen vorbehalten. Zwischenzeitlich versteckten auch die Zürcher ihre öffentlichen Toiletten, doch heute ist der Stolz wieder da: Schnittige Anlagen aus den 1920er Jahren werden sorgfältig restauriert und erst vor kurzem verabschiedete der Stadtrat den »Masterplan ZüriWC«, um die knapp 100 Einrichtungen auf den neusten Stand zu bringen. Von den modernsten Anlagen Europas ist die Rede, teilweise mit Duschen ausgestattet, und es geht das Gerücht, der damalige New Yorker Bürgermeister Rudolph Giuliani hätte im Sommer 2000 auf einem Zürcher Klo sitzend entschieden, seiner Stadt auch 200 neue zu bescheren.

Modern, sauber und zahlreich – was will man mehr? Aber seien wir ehrlich: Unter der Erde, dahin, wo das prüde 20. Jahrhundert den öffentlichen Abort verbannt hat, ist die Entleerung nicht nur unsicher, sondern auch freudlos. Die etymologische Herleitung des Wortes Latrine von *latere* (verborgen sein) ist erwiesenermaßen falsch und von Kindesbeinen an hat der Blick in die freie Natur einen magisch-anregenden Einfluss auf die Verdauungstätigkeit des Blickenden.

Nicht umsonst trafen sich Ende des 18. Jahrhunderts täglich hunderte von Parisern, um hinter den Hecken der Tuilerien abzuhocken, bis der Adel

in a similarly proud style. Around 1900 urinals in front of church portals were even a part of the everyday picture – this would have been unthinkable in Catholic Vienna. It was not until the 1930's that the authorities here managed to acquire the approval for a convenience to meet the respective needs of the passers-by at Stephansplatz – even if only underground and indicated by a prude signpost with "Here" on it. In Zurich the town-planners themselves designed the public conveniences. Partially in prominent urban locations, horns of plenty decorate their entrance, with clocks chiming over the top – these otherwise being reserved for other significant buildings such as churches or train stations. For a while, the Zurich population also hid their public toilets, but today they have regained their pride: Elegant places dating back to the 1920's are being carefully renovated and just recently the town council approved the "Masterplan ZüriWC", for modernising their conveniences, totalling almost 100. Concerned here are the most up-to-date systems in Europe, some of them equipped with showers, and as the rumour goes, the former Mayor of New York, Rudolph Giuliani decided whilst sitting on the loo in Zurich in the summer of 2000, to offer his town 200 more.

Modern, clean and plentiful – what more could you want? But let's be honest: Down underground, where the prude 20th century banished the public lavatory, emptying one's bowels is not only a precarious business but also devoid of any pleasure. Deriving the word "latrine" from *latere* (being hidden) is etymologically incorrect. Besides, a view into the open countryside from childhood onwards has a magical, stimulating effect on the digestive activity of the person involved.

It was not without reason that at the end of the 18th century hundreds of Parisians met daily to crouch behind the hedges of the Tuileries Gardens, until the nobility could not bear the stench any longer and had the yew tree pulled out. On the Ring Road in Vienna two "tree keepers" kept guard from 1868 onwards as the plane-trees did not want to flourish next to the urinals set up there. Everywhere the people preferred to relieve nature out in the open instead of in obligatory cramped facilities. At the Berlin Love Parade 2000, the ecosystem of the "Tiergarten" almost broke down because of some million ravers who used the hundreds of Dixi loos as bleacher seats, and thereby transforming the park into a toilet.

The desire to relieve nature in the open air was indeed prohibited at an early stage, but when dealt with in an artistic way, it also gave rise to many a pretty room. The splendid latrines at the time of the Roman Empire were large, lavishly equipped rooms, where up to 80 persons congregated to empty their bowels. Sitting in a rectangle or semi-circle, the wealthy gentlemen gazed out into an open courtyard with splashing water basins. Running water additionally washed away one's business underneath the seat, keeping the air fresh. In places without any open space a pictorial substitute was provided for. Archaeologists found a latrine vault in a Roman cellar painted with twigs of lemon trees, fig trees and song-birds – which only goes to show that the desire for freshness and open-air could not have been exclusively for hygienic reasons. According to Seneca, virtue frequents open places and lust, musty rooms.

These are seldom found, but in our modern times there are also adequate examples. For in-

den Gestank nicht mehr ertrug und den Taxus ausreißen ließ. Auf der Wiener Ringstraße schoben ab 1868 zwei »Baumwärter« Wache, da die Platanen, neben den neu erstellten Pissoirs, nicht recht gedeihen wollten. Überall zog man es vor, sich weiterhin unter freiem Himmel zu erleichtern, statt in den engen, vorgeschriebenen Behältnissen. Bei der Berliner Loveparade 2000 kippte fast das Ökosystem des Tiergartens, weil einige Millionen Raver hunderte Dixi-Klos als Logenplatz umfunktionierten und den Park zur Toilette.

Der Sehnsucht nach Entleerung im Freien wurde zwar schon früh ein Riegel vorgeschoben, künstlerisch umgesetzt, brachte sie jedoch gleichzeitig manch schönen Raum hervor. Die Prachtlatrinen der römischen Kaiserzeit waren große, mit üppigen Materialien ausgestattete Räume, in denen sich bis zu 80 Personen zum gemeinsamen Stuhlgang einfanden. Im Rechteck oder Halbrund sitzend, blickten die wohlhabenden Herren in einen lichten Hof mit plätschernden Wasserbecken. Fließendes Wasser spülte außerdem unter dem Sitz das Geschäft fort und klärte die Luft. Wo die räumliche Offenheit fehlte, sorgte man für bildlichen Ersatz: So fanden Archäologen in einem römischen Keller ein Latrinengewölbe, bemalt mit Zweigen von Zitronen- und Feigenbäumen und Singvögeln – was zeigt, dass der Wunsch nach Frische und Öffnung nicht ausschließlich hygienische Gründe haben konnte: Laut Seneca hält sich die Tugend im Freien auf und die Wollust in muffigen Räumen.

Sie sind zwar selten, aber auch in der Neuzeit finden sich adäquate Beispiele. So beschrieb der englische Satiriker Jonathan Swift 1743 eine fiktive öffentliche Bedürfnisanstalt, auf deren Boden man im Winter türkische Teppiche ausbreitet und im Sommer Blumen und Laub streut. Die unterirdische Anlage am Wiener Graben ist das schönste Beispiel der Prachtentfaltung mit der die Belle Epoque den Ort des Stuhlgangs in eine angenehmere Atmosphäre tauchen wollte: Neben Schiebetüren aus Eiche und Klobrillen aus Teak glänzten Messing und Majolika. Höhepunkt war auch hier ein Natursurrogat: zwei mit Goldfischen und Eidechsen bevölkerte Aquarien mit Springbrunnen, gerahmt von üppigem Blumenschmuck.

Diese Toilette in Wien ist, ebenso wie die Überreste der römischen Prachtlatrinen, heute eine Sehenswürdigkeit. Sucht man in unserer Zeit nach Klos, die in hundert Jahren Touristen erfreuen könnten, hat man ein Problem. Lediglich die Pressemeldung von einer neuen öffentlichen

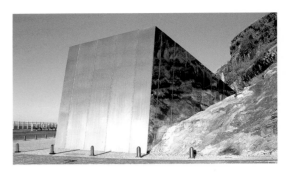

Der französische Architekt
Robert Latour d'Affaure baute
2001 eine WC-Anlage in San
Sebastián, Spanien. Wie ein
verspiegelter Monolith ragt die
öffentliche Toilette aus dem
baskischen Felsen. Zugang
zum erratischen Block gewährt
eine Drehtür, die von innen
Blicke aufs Meer und den Horizont freigibt.

The French architect Robert
Latour d'Affaure built a public
convenience in 2001 in San
Sebastián, Spain. Like a reflecting monolith this public
toilet towers from the Basque
rock. Entrance to the erratic
block is through a revolving
door displaying a view of the
sea and the horizon from the
interior.

Die 2002 fertiggestellte Toilette im alten Hafen von Dubrovnik, Kroatien, schmiegt sich an das Gebäude der Hafenverwaltung aus den Zeiten der Habsburger Monarchie. Gleichzeitig öffnete der Architekt Nenad Fabijanić mit seinem steinernen, langgestreckten Gebäude eine neue Passage entlang der Stadtmauer. Nachts erhellen Bodenstrahler den Weg und tauchen den Bau in sanftes Licht.

The public toilet in the old port of Dubrovnik in Croatia, finished in 2002, nestles against the port administration building dating back to the Habsburgs. At the same time, the architect Nenad Fabijanić opened a new footway along the town walls with his long stretch of stone building. At night, ground lamps light up the way and immerse the building in a gentle glow.

»4-Sterne-Toilette« in der Verbotenen Stadt Pekings lässt aufhorchen: »ein Prachtstück, das Klimaanlage, Ruheraum mit Sofa und Bar sowie einen Fernseher von 23 Zoll bietet, wahrhaft kaiserlich. An spiegelnden Kachelwänden Gemälde und Kalligrafie, Plastikefeu sorgt für Grün.« Dass die 4 700 Gassenklohäuschen der Stadt eine dürftigere Ausstattung haben, ahnt man, wenn man weiß, dass nahezu die Hälfte der Chinesen kein eigenes Klo besitzen. Sie sitzen stattdessen, wie die alten Römer, dicht an dicht, Trennwände fehlen.

Ob auf den Latrinen von Peking die morgendliche Unterhaltung blüht? Die Geselligkeit spielte lange Zeit eine wichtige Rolle beim gemeinsamen Stuhlgang. Die Römer diskutierten ausgiebig. Die klassischen Philosophendispute sollen sogar der kommunikativen halbrunden Form der frühen Athener Latrine als Anregung gedient haben. Schließlich führen noch heute Männer tiefschürfende Gespräche vor der Piss-Rinne.

Was das Klo als Ort des Austauschs leisten kann, machen uns die Schwulen vor. Seit hundert Jahren ist die Bedürfnisanstalt ein fester Bestandteil ihrer Szene. Hier gesellt sich Mann zu Mann, schaut und greift, bei Gefallen, zu. Doch der Siegeszug der Automatiktoilette wird wohl jegliche Art sexueller oder anderer Begegnung an solchen Orten unwahrscheinlich machen – nach 15 Minuten öffnet sich die Tür, bei über 100 Kilogramm Belastung schließt sie erst gar nicht. In Paris sind zudem alle »Sanisette« nach 22 Uhr nicht mehr in Betrieb.

Lustfeindliche Welt! Noch vor gar nicht allzu langer Zeit schrieb Henry Miller, dass der Anblick der Pariser Pissoirs ihn »bis in die Eingeweide erregt und erwärmt«. Beim Anblick einer vollautomatischen Bedürfnisbox meint man nur noch, den Geschmack von Desinfektionsmittel im Mund zu spüren. Doch es gibt sie noch, die guten Dinge! Unter dem Motto »Competence in Shit« brachte der Amerikaner Fred Edwards vor dreißig Jahren die mobile Toilettenkabine nach Europa. Das klassische Dixi-Klo – blau-braun mit Satteldach und weißem Herzlein an der Tür – ist so etwas wie die Urhütte des Abortes aus Plastik. Durch die seitlichen Lüftungsschlitze in Augenhöhe blickt der Pinkler auf das Geschehen rundum, und lässt sich das Absitzen nicht vermeiden, leistet das Busengirl von Seite eins Gesellschaft, von einem Bauarbeiter freundlicherweise zurückgelassen. An einem solchen Ort keimt die Hoffnung, dass wir das Potenzial des öffentlichen Klos neu entdecken – nicht für das hygienische Verrichten einer Notdurft, sondern für ein lustvolles Entleeren mit beiläufigen Erlebnissen.

stance, the English satirist Jonathan Swift described a fictive public convenience in 1743, where Turkish carpets were laid on the floor in the winter and in the summer was strewed with flowers and foliage. The underground convenience at Vienna's "Graben" is the most beautiful example of the unfolding splendour with which the Belle Epoque wanted to plunge the place for relieving nature into a pleasant atmosphere. Besides oak push-doors and teak lavatory seats, bronze and majolica gleam. Here, too, the highlight played a surrogate role for a natural environment – two aquariums inhabited by goldfish and newts with fountains, adorned with luxurious floral decorations.

Today, this toilet in Vienna is a tourist sight, just like the remains of the splendiferous Roman latrines. Anyone searching for a public convenience built in our time that would be able to please tourists in a hundred years, would have a problem. Merely the press announcements about a new public "4 star toilet" in the Forbidden City of Peking arouse our interest – "a splendid place offering air-conditioning, a restroom with couch and bar, as well as a 23" TV – truly fit for a king. Paintings and calligraphy on reflecting tiled walls with plastic ivy providing the greenery." Knowing that almost half the Chinese do not have their own toilet, one suspects that the 4,700 back-street toilets in the town have less adequate furnishings. Instead, they sit shoulder to shoulder like the old Romans without any dividing walls.

I wonder whether morning entertainment flourishes on the latrines in Peking? Companionship during communal "bowel motion" played an important role for a long while. The Romans held lengthy discussions. The communicative

semi-circular form of the early Athenian latrine is even said to have served for stimulating the disputes of classic philosophers. After all, men still hold lengthy conversations at the pissoir today.

The gays demonstrate how the toilet can be used as a place for communication. For one hundred years, the conveniences have been an integral part of their scene. Here, man meets man, watches, and if he wishes to, takes hold of it. Yet the triumphal march of the automatic toilet will render any form of sexual, or other meeting at such places improbable – after 15 minutes the door opens and does not even shut if 100 kg are exceeded. Moreover, in Paris none of the "Sanisettes" are in operation any later than 10 p.m.

What a prudish world! And it was not so long ago that Henry Miller wrote that the sight of a Parisian pissoir stimulated and warmed him to the visceral nerves. When looking at a fully automatic toilet cell one only has an aseptic taste in one's mouth. But they still exists, the dear things! Under the motto "Competence in Shit" the American Fred Edwards brought the mobile toilet cell to Europe thirty years ago. The classic Dixi loo – blue/brown with a saddled roof and a little white heart on the door – something like the primeval WC in plastic. Through the slit at the side at eye-level, the pisser can view what is going on all round and if having to sit down to do one's business cannot be avoided, the bosomy girl on the front page, kindly left behind by a construction worker, keeps him company. At a place like this hope is budding for re-discovering the potential of public conveniences – not for the hygienic purpose of relieving nature but for enjoyably emptying the bowels with incidental adventure thrown in.

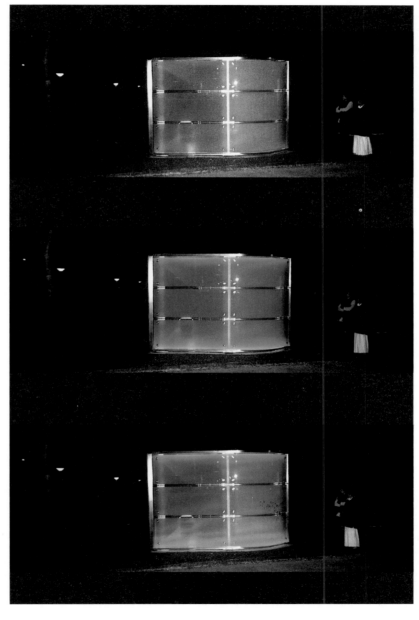

In verschiedenen Farben funkelt die gläserne Hülle des skulptural wirkenden Klo-Juwels, entwickelt von Hans Ulrich Imesch. Im Prototypen der öffentlichen Bedürfnisanstalt können sich Sankt Galler seit 2001 erleichtern.

The glass exterior of the sculpture-type jewel WC, created by Hans Ulrich Imesch, sparkles in different colours. The people in St. Gallen have been able to relieve themselves in the prototype of the public convenience since 2001.

Badelust in Island

An Icelandic park for bathing

Olga Gudrún Sigfússdóttir

In einem Badepark am Myvatn im Norden Islands soll die Tradition des Badens in heißen Quellen in neuer Form aufblühen.

A design for a bathing park near Lake Myvatn, north Iceland, continues the tradition of hot springs bathing in new ways.

Die Badekultur in Island hat eine lange Tradition. Es gibt zahlreiche natürliche Quellen, die überwiegend in der Vulkanzone Islands liegen. Seit der Besiedlung des Landes nutzten die Menschen diese Naturquellen und bauten sie zu bequemen Bädern aus, wie die Islandsagas und alte Erzählungen berichten. Die so entstandene Badekultur war unvergleichlich, da es sich fast nur um natürliche Bäder in freier Natur handelte, Bäder ohne Infrastruktur und Komfort. Die Badekultur heute hat sich aber weit von ihrem Ursprung entfernt. Dennoch sind einige historische Badearten bis heute erhalten geblieben. Überliefert sind das Dampfbad, das Sandbad, der heiße Pool und die Badestelle.

Projektgebiet Myvatn in Nordisland. Das Naturschutzgebiet Myvatn liegt inmitten der vulkanischen Landschaft mit dem Vulkan Krafla, einem der aktivsten der Insel. Erdbeben sind daher häufig und überall gibt es Zeugen dafür, dass sich die Kontinentalplatten verschieben. Manche Erdspalten sind bis zu 100 Kilometer lang.

Das Planungsgebiet Bjarnaflag, in dem viele heiße Quellen entspringen, liegt östlich der Ortschaft Reykjahlid. Bislang wird die Erdwärme dort hauptsächlich zur Energiegewinnung für die zwei Fabriken am Ort genutzt. Das Gebiet Bjarnaflag war von der Besiedlung des Landes an ein Badeort. Hier die alte isländische Badekultur wiederzubeleben, ist das Hauptziel des Entwurfes. Das Gebiet Bjarnaflag stellt sich als problematisch dar, da es keine klaren Grenzen aufweist und die überwältigende Natur an dieser Stelle keine maßstabsbildenden Elemente bereithält. Einer Kraterlandschaft auf dem Mond ähnelt der Ort. Ein architektonischer Eingriff an dieser Stelle muss sich in jedem Fall der Natur unterordnen, möchte er nicht das Bild und die Wirkung der Landschaft zerstören.

Am Anfang des Entwurfsprozesses steht die Analyse des Gebietes unter geologischen und infrastrukturellen Aspekten. An verschiedenen Stellen existiert Erdwärme in unterschiedlichen Formen, die zwar natürlich erscheinen, wie die Lagune und der warme Fluss, die sich jedoch bei näherer Betrachtung teilweise als durch menschlichen Eingriff entstanden erweisen. Bedingt durch unterirdische heiße Quellen entsteht Dampf, der aus Erdlöchern und Spalten hervorströmt oder durch den Sand dringt. Ruinen alter Badestellen zeugen davon, dass der Dampf schon früher zum

Bathing culture has a long tradition in Iceland. The country has countless natural springs, most of them located in the country's volcanic zone. Since the days when man began to settle the country, people have used the springs for bathing. The bathing culture was unique in that it mainly involved natural baths located out in the open, equipped with nothing in the way of infrastructure or amenities. Although modern approaches to bathing on the island have little in common with the past, some historical means are still in use, such as bathing in steam, sand, hot pools, and crevice pools.

The Lake Myvatn area in north Iceland. The character of the Lake Myvatn conservation area is largely determined by the volcanic landscape. This includes the Krafla volcano, one of the most active in Iceland. Earthquakes occur frequently, and rifts and faults resulting from the drift of the continental plates, and reaching 100 kilometres in length, can be seen everywhere. The Bjarnaflag planning area, where many hot springs exist, is located east of the village of Reykjahlid, and the subterranean geothermal energy is used to power two factories. Vents emitting hot gases and vapours have been used for steam baths in the area since the land was settled, and thus the main objective of a dissertation design for a bathing park in Bjarnaflag is to revive Iceland's ancient bathing culture. Planning the insertion of bathing stations into the Bjarnaflag area proved to be problematic since it is comparable to a crater landscape on the moon and does not offer clearly delineated structures or any sense of scale. In other words, care had to be taken to fit the architectural interventions into the surroundings to avoid ruining the appearance of the volcanic terrain.

66

The design process began with an analysis of the area in terms of its geology and infrastructure. Geothermal energy is in evidence in various forms that seem natural in origin, but which, as in the case of a lagoon and a hot water course, prove to be a side-effect of man-made interventions. In contrast, the steam emerging through holes and cracks in the ground or making its way up through sand is the result of naturally occurring subterranean hot springs. Ruins of old abandoned bathing places indicate that steam has long been used for bathing at the location.

The Bjarnaflag area also features industrial installations, such as a diatomite factory and a stone works, which stand in strange contrast to the fact that they are located in a nature conservation area. However, the factories were built in the days before the area was given protected status, and not only do they use the geothermal energy of the hot springs, but their emissions are not toxic, either.

The park and reception building. The dissertation design suggests creating a bathing park in the area, which is marked by the contrast of nature and technology, spectacular scenery and old industrial installations, and providing it with small natural bathing units supplied with water or steam from natural hot springs on the one hand, and with industrial process water from the industrial installations on the other. Accordingly, the design seeks to fit the bathing stations into the landscape to reconcile these differences. The plan includes a footpath system to link the individual stations in the path while providing visitors with a more immediate experience of the volcanic landscape. The park itself is designed at 500 x 1,800 metres in size, and is crossed in the north by a country road. This presents an ideal location

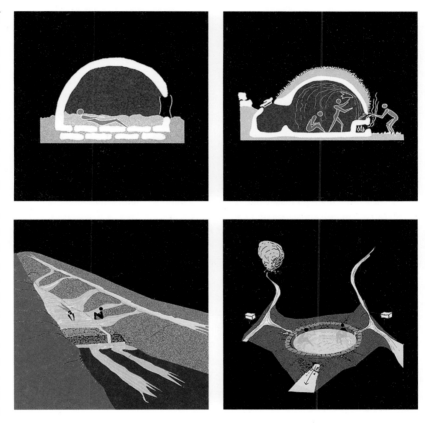

Baden benutzt worden ist. Widersprüchlich scheinen zunächst die industriellen Anlagen im Planungsgebiet, wie die Kieselerdefabrik oder die Steinfabrik inmitten des Naturschutzgebietes. Die Fabriken, welche aus der Zeit stammen, als der Ort noch nicht unter Naturschutz stand, nutzen die Erdwärme der heißen Quellen, ihre Emissionen sind ungiftig.

Der Park und der Empfangsbereich. Im Spannungsfeld von Natur und Technik, von überwältigender Landschaft und alten Industrieanlagen soll ein neuer Badepark, mit kleinen Einheiten verschiedener Badeanlagen, entstehen, die zum einen durch die natürlichen heißen Dampfquellen versorgt, zum anderen vom warmen Brauchwasser der Fabriken gespeist werden. Der Vorschlag sieht vor, Badehäuser als vermittelndes Element in

die Landschaft einzufügen, mit einem Wanderweg die einzelnen Stationen im Park miteinander zu verbinden und die Landschaft wieder erlebbar zu machen. Der Park erstreckt sich über eine Fläche von etwa 500 mal 1 800 Metern. Im Norden zerteilt eine Landstraße das Areal in zwei Hälften. Dort sind der Parkplatz, der Empfang mit Information, Kasse und Cafeteria sowie der Ausgangspunkt der Wanderwege vorgesehen. Ein Rundweg soll nördlich um die Lagune herum führen, der andere nach Süden und an einer Erdspalte enden, einem geeigneten Ort für das Schluchtbad. Den Weg zwischen den Stationen könnten maßstabsbildende vertikale Elemente markieren, Mauern oder Stangen. Diese Objekte stehen im Kontrast zur Landschaft und sollen den Raum definieren. Die Badestationen erreicht man nur zu Fuß, die größte Entfernung, vom Empfangsgebäude bis zum Schluchtbad, beträgt etwa 1,5 Kilometer. Die einzelnen Wegabschnitte sollen unterschiedlich ausgeformt werden und direkten Bezug auf die jeweiligen Badeanlagen nehmen sowie auf die Besonderheit der Landschaft.

Die Badestationen. Für den Badepark sieht der Entwurf fünf verschiedene Typen von Badeanlagen vor. Ihr Standort wird durch die vorhandenen Quellen bestimmt: Das Lagunenbad liegt an der grünen Lagune, die vom Brauchwasser der Kieselerdefabrik gespeist wird; das Dampfbad wird

for a car park, a reception building and a cafeteria. The park trails start at this building, one of them leading to the north and around the lagoon, and the other to the south, where it ends at the crevice pool. The bathing stations are intended to be only accessible by foot and the greatest distance involved, namely that from the reception building to the crevice pool, is about one and a half kilometres. The individual sections of path refer in character to the bathing stations to which they lead and the particular qualities of the immediate surroundings.

The bathing stations. The plan suggests five different types of bathing facilities, most of them at sites where warm water or steam occur naturally. It situates the steam bath above a steam vent, the sand bath at a place where steam percolates up through sand, and the crevice bath at a natural crevice filled by a pool of hot water. The lagoon bath is placed on the green lagoon formed

by process water from the diatomite factory, and the river bath at the process water outlet of a planned geothermal power plant.

The lagoon bath. The green lagoon is located at the northern edge of the park, and holds process water 38 to 42 degrees Celsius in temperature. The green-blue diatom algae in the water are said to be beneficial to sufferers of skin complaints. Until now, it has only been possible to bathe in the lagoon on warm summer days, but the bathing pavilion would make this possible in all weathers. In the design, the pavilion is given the form of an elongated structure reaching into the water from the shore. A double row of columns form the front wall in the water to provide bathers with direct access to the warm lagoon. Inside, the facility is reduced to a minimum in the way of amenities, simply offering showers and changing rooms, and has the appearance of a flowing space between the inside and the outside.

auf heiße Dampfquellen gesetzt; das gleiche gilt für das Sandbad, bei dem der Dampf durch den Sand gefiltert wird; das Flussbad liegt am Brauchwasserabfluss des geplanten Geothermalkraftwerkes; das Schluchtbad macht sich das Warmwasservorkommen in einer Erdspalte zu Nutze.

Das Lagunenbad. Am nördlichen Rand des Parks liegt die grüne Lagune, ein Brauchwassersee, dessen Temperatur 38 bis 42 Grad Celsius beträgt. Eine Besonderheit stellen die grünblauen Kieselalgen dar, denen eine heilende Wirkung bei Hautkrankheiten zugesprochen wird. Bislang konnte man dort nur an warmen Sommertagen baden. Der neue Pavillon könnte das Baden bei jeder Witterung ermöglichen. Von außen präsentiert sich das Lagunenbad als geschlossener langgestreckter Baukörper, der vom Ufer ins Wasser ragt. An der Frontseite im Wasser bricht die Geschlossenheit der Fassade durch eine doppelschichtige Stelenwand auf. Der Baukörper löst sich auf und ermöglicht dem Badenden den Weg zum offenen Wasser. Von innen zeigt sich das Bad mit seinen auf ein Minimum reduzierten Funktionen wie Dusche und Umkleide als fließender Raum zwischen Innen und Außen.

Das Dampfbad. Das Baden im Dampf hat die längste Tradition am Ort. Das Dampfbad ist als länglicher Baukörper geplant, der sich den unterirdischen Quellen entgegen in den Boden gräbt. Durch den Eingang an der Stirnseite betritt der Besucher das Bad und überwindet das leichte

Ein Muss für jeden Naturbad-Freund ist Landmannalaugar. Die heißen Quellen des Lavafeldes Laugahraun speisen wundervoll gelegene Teiche. Eine einfache Plattform reicht als Umkleidemöglichkeit.

Landmannalaugar, where the hot and cold springs of the Laugahraun lava field create natural pools in the landscape, is a must for all friends of open-air bathing. A platform is all that is needed for changing.

Gefälle über einzelne Treppenstufen hinunter bis zur eigentlichen Dampfbadekabine. Auf dem Weg nach unten durchquert er dabei, einem linearen Ablauf folgend, Umkleidezone und Dusche. Der Baderaum ist nahezu quadratisch angelegt und sitzt genau über einem Erdloch, aus dem heißer Dampf aufsteigt. Der Dampf entweicht über eine Öffnung in der Decke. Dem Baderaum vorgelagert ist ein Ruheraum. Abkühlung erfährt der Badende, wenn er durch eine Tür an der Seite ins Freie tritt. Die Temperatur des Dampfes in der Badekabine beträgt etwa 60 Grad Celsius, die Luftfeuchtigkeit 90 Prozent.

Das Flussbad. Das Flussbad entspricht dem historischen Baden im heißen Pool. An einem Geländesprung wird der Brauchwasserabfluss des Geothermalkraftwerkes in einem Becken gestaut und dann durch Öffnungen in der Stauwand als künstlicher Wasserfall in das Gebäude geleitet. Hier mündet er in einem Badebecken unter freiem Himmel. Die Badeanlage ist an der Stelle geplant, wo das Wasser eine angenehme Temperatur zum Baden hat, etwa 40 bis 42 Grad Celsius, und bevor es wieder im Boden ver- schwindet. Das Baden im fließenden Wasser symbolisiert die Rein- waschung und das be- freiende Abfließen jeg- lichen Schmutzes.

The steam baths. Steam baths have the longest tradition at Bjarnaflag. The respective facility is planned as a long building that disappears into the ground towards the subterranean springs. Visitors would enter the baths through the en- trance in the end wall, and walk down a few steps to overcome the difference in elevation on the way to the steam bath cabins. The downward path leads past a linear arrangement made up of a changing zone and showers. The bathing room is almost square in shape and located directly above a vent in the earth from which hot steam emerges before eventually escaping through a hole in the roof. A rest room is located in front of the bathing room, and a side door would enable visitors to cool down by stepping outside into the fresh air. The temperature in the steam cabins would be about 60 degrees Celsius and humidity about 90 percent.

The brook pool. The brook bathing place would enable a form of bathing similar to tradi- tional bathing in hot pools. The plan suggests capturing process water produced by the power plant into a pool, and leading it through an open- ing in the far wall, down into an open-air swim- ming pool. The brook consists of a course of cleansed process water produced by the planned

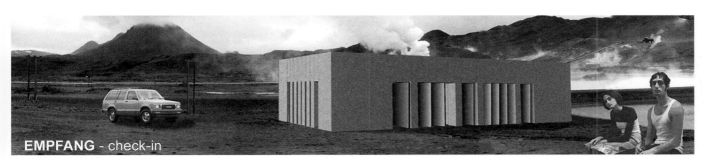

EMPFANG - check-in

Ein kleiner Pavillon dient als Empfangsgebäude für den vorgeschlagenen Badepark. Dort starten die Wege zu den einzelnen Badestationen. Wegmarken entlang dieser Pfade, zum Beispiel in den Fels geschlagene Treppen (unten), orientieren sich an alten Vorbildern. Einst wiesen Steinpyramiden den Reitern den Weg durch das Land (unten links).

A small pavilion serves as a reception and amenities building for the proposed bathing park, and is also the starting point for the trails leading to the individual bathing stations. Path-side elements, such as steps hewn into the rock (below), take their inspiration from the past, when pyramids of stone used to guide riders on their way through the barren landscape (below left).

geothermal power plant. The bathing facility would best be located at the place where the water reaches an appropriate temperature for bathing – namely 40 to 42 degrees Celsius – before disappearing into the ground.

The crevice pool. A natural pool of hot water has been discovered in a crevice on the southern edge of the park, enabling a form of bathing that goes back a long way in time, far removed from the influences of civilisation. Accordingly, in adapting the crevice for public bathing, the dissertation uses a minimum of man-made elements to ensure as little interference with the natural experience as possible. The suggested arrangement of smooth concrete panels on the wall symbolises the movement of the continental plates, and forms a contrast to the rough walls of the crevice. One of the panels juts out of the crevice, thus marking its location in the landscape. The design includes a stepway that leads down from a platform on slide bearings to a bathing platform, where visitors undress behind simple partitions. The crystal-clear water in the pool would be about 40 degrees Celsius, and it is likely that by the time people got down to the pool, they would want to remain in it for a long time, since bathing in crevices is regarded as particularly relaxing.

Das Schluchtbad. In einer Erdspalte am südlichen Rand des Parks hat man ein warmes Wasservorkommen entdeckt, das den Grund der Spalte füllt. In der Tiefe der Schlucht soll man ursprünglich, fernab jeder Zivilisation Baden können. Die Intervention ist auf ein Minimum reduziert, um an dieser Stelle die Macht der Natur spürbar zu machen. Betonscheiben, die an den Schluchtwänden befestigt sind, betonen die Bewegung der Kontinentalplatten, und die rauen Wände der Schlucht werden durch die glatten Scheiben kontrastiert. Eine der Scheiben ragt aus der Schlucht heraus und markiert damit die Badeanlage in der Landschaft. Von einer Plattform auf Gleitlagern führt eine Treppe hinunter zu einer Badeplattform. Hinter einfachen Paravents kann der Besucher sich umkleiden. Das kristallklare Wasser ist etwa 40 Grad Celsius warm. Wenn man es schließlich erreicht hat, verweilt man gerne. Das Bad in der Schlucht gilt als besonders entspannend.

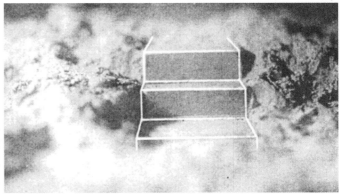

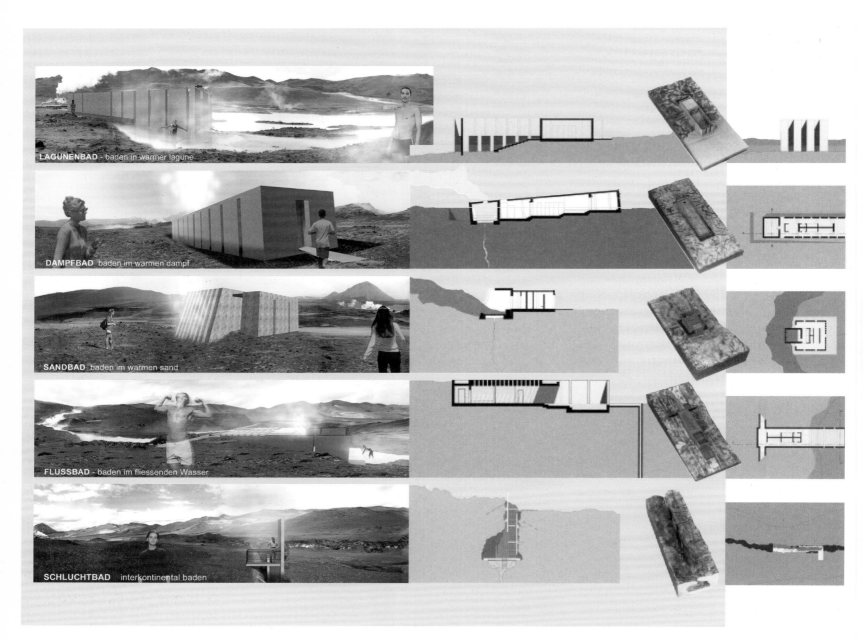

LAGUNENBAD - baden in warmer lagune

DAMPFBAD baden im warmen dampf

SANDBAD baden im warmen sand

FLUSSBAD - baden im fliessenden Wasser

SCHLUCHTBAD interkontinental baden

Kleine Badehäuser, eingepasst in die Vulkanlandschaft, könnten traditionellen Badegenuss in moderner Architektur bieten (von oben nach unten): Plantschen in der Lagune, Schwitzen im Dampfbad, Entspannen im Sandbad, Schwimmen im Flussbad und unterirdisches Eintauchen im Schluchtbad.

Small bathhouses fitted into the volcanic landscape are a possible means of enabling traditional bathing forms in contemporary architecture. Top down: Lagoon for splashing about; steam bath for a good sweat; sand bath for pure relaxation; a dammed pool for swimming, and a crevice pool for underground bathing.

Kleine Bauten in großartiger Umgebung

Small structures in the big Finnish outdoors

A building is always a statement. No matter how large, it is always a sign of the presence of man, to say the least. The more natural the environment it stands in, the more this applies. Inserting a building into a natural environment raises ethical questions: Do we have the right to submit ever-increasing areas of nature to our influence? Do buildings really lead to something better? In areas already displaying the human touch, this is not such a problem, but nevertheless the question remains: do we really need more buildings?

Since nature is not improved by man-made additions, we have to consider the benefits of building activities from our point of view, and in this respect it must be admitted that the marriage of architecture and nature can create moments of beauty and delight. In approaching new projects, it has to be considered whether the building will be a central or secondary element in its surroundings. Certain rules have to be followed in the design of free-standing structures on unbuilt sites; although it has to be admitted that abandoning the rules often results in impressive architecture. Nonetheless, this cannot be taken as a design principle, since the result would be an environment of endless attempts and little success. Thus while the challenges confronting the designer are numerous, the fruits of tackling the challenges can be poetic.

Transparency of building volume, lightness of construction and harmonious surface materials and colours are key issues in trying to adjust a building to its surroundings. Traditional materials like stone, wood, steel and glass blend in harmoniously in contrast to refined industrial materials, which often lack the ability to age gracefully.

Ein Gebäude ist immer ein Statement. Zumindest stellen Bauten, unabhängig von ihrer Größe, ein Zeichen menschlicher Präsenz dar. Je natürlicher die Umgebung, umso stärker wirkt die Botschaft. Beim Arbeiten in natürlichem Terrain stellen sich moralische Fragen: Haben wir das Recht, immer größere Gebiete zu bebauen, führen immer mehr Gebäude zu etwas Besserem? In Gebieten, die bereits von menschlichen Eingriffen dominiert werden, gibt es dieses Dilemma nicht, aber die Grundfrage bleibt: Brauchen wir mehr Gebäude?

Da die Natur selbst nie durch menschengemachte Beiträge verbessert wird, kann der Vorteil der Bauaktivität nur von einem egoistischen Standpunkt aus betrachtet werden. Akzeptiert man dies, gibt es einige Projekte, die durch die Vereinigung von Architektur und Natur, Momente der Schönheit und der Freude schaffen. Eine Hauptentscheidung bei neuen Bauprojekten ist, ob das Gebäude zentraler Blickpunkt werden soll oder sich als zweitrangiges Element in seiner Umgebung im Hintergrund hält. Es gibt sicherlich Regeln beim Gestalten von freistehenden Bauten auf unbebautem Gelände, wobei eingeräumt werden muss, dass eindrucksvolle Architektur oft entsteht, wenn Regeln missachtet werden. Dies kann allerdings keine Gestaltungsleitlinie sein, da das Ergebnis eine Lebensumwelt endloser Versuche mit wenig Erfolg sein würde. Die Früchte der Auseinandersetzung mit diesem Problem können durchaus poetisch sein.

Transparenz des Bauvolumens, Leichtigkeit der Konstruktion, Harmonie der Oberflächenmaterialien und Farben sind Schlüsselpunkte beim erfolgreichen Anpassen an die Umgebung. Traditionelle Materialien wie Stein, Holz, Stahl und Glas fügen sich harmonisch ein, im Gegensatz zu veredelten industriellen Materialien, denen oft die Fähigkeit fehlt, anmutig zu altern. Das tägliche Spiel von Licht und Schatten ist essentiell für die Architektur genauso wie in der Natur. Dies in Verbindung mit dem langsamen Wechsel der Jahreszeiten und immer wieder wechselndem Wetter gibt uns die Möglichkeit, Architektur mit der vierten Dimension, der Zeit, zu verbinden.

Der Winter bringt einen besonderen Aspekt für die finnische Landschaft. Das Erscheinungsbild von Gebäuden und Landschaft wirkt unter einer Schneedecke total verändert. Die Lasten, verursacht vom Gewicht schmelzenden Schnees,

Roy Mänttäri

Drei kleine Nutzbauten in Finnland setzen Zeichen in der Landschaft, ohne den Kontext zur Umgebung zu negieren.

Three small structures demonstrate a powerful presence without negating the character of their surroundings.

Der Architekt Ville Hara entwarf einen Aussichtsturm für den Zoo von Helsinki auf der Insel Korkeasaari. Die blasenförmige Holzkonstruktion steht an einem exponierten felsigen Ort auf der Insel. 2002 fertiggestellt, avancierte sie zur markanten Landmarke.

The architect Ville Hara designed a lookout tower for Korkeasaari Zoo in Helsinki. The eye-shaped wooden structure is sited conspicuously on a prominent bedrock promontory on the western edge of the zoo island. Completed in 2002, it has since become a striking landmark.

sind ein wichtiger Faktor bei statischen Überlegungen, die in schwereren Konstruktionen münden als in südlicheren Lagen. Schnee ist bestimmt ein ästhetischer Segen, der die Szenerie magisch verändert. Dieses Phänomen bietet eine wundervolle Möglichkeit für Architektur und Landschaftsarchitektur, die bedauerlicherweise viel zu selten genutzt wird.

Zwei der hier präsentierten kleinen Bauten finden sich am Stadtrand, einer auf dem Lande. Alle drei sollen einerseits bestimmten Nutzungen dienen, sich andererseits gleichzeitig in der Umgebung auflösen. Keine der drei Lösungen folgt traditionellen Modellen, sondern vertraut auf den direkten Einfluss des Geländes.

Aussichtsturm. Der aufsehenerregende Bau steht auf einem markanten Felsen am Westrand von Helsinki, der Zooinsel Korkeasaari. Die Holzkonstruktion ist transparent und bildet gleichzeitig ein Volumen. Das Gitter erinnert an die eingesperrten Tiere im Zoo, während die Blasen-Form einem Auge gleicht, ein passendes Symbol für eine Aussichtsplattform. Der schwere felsige Untergrund und der luftig leichte Bau schaffen eine visuelle Spannung. Im Laufe der Zeit wird die frische bräunliche Farbe des Holzes grau werden und sich der umgebenden Betonmauer und dem oft grauen Farbton des Himmels einfügen. Die organische Form erlaubt ein angemessenes Verhältnis zur Landschaft, trotz der zwangsläufig auffallenden Lage.

Der Sockel des Turms kann leider weniger überzeugen als das Gesamtkonzept. Die unklare Form der Randsteine kontrastiert mit der Klarheit des Turms und schnürt den Optimismus des Turms mit konventioneller Langeweile ein. Eine einfachere Herangehensweise hätte sicherlich die Gesamtidee besser unterstützt.

Lusthäuschen. Die winzige Hütte steht in scheinbar unberührter Natur, in einer archetypischen finnischen Szenerie aus Seen und Wäldern. Das Gelände ist ein felsiger Hügel mit kargem, trockenem Boden und schütteren Kiefern. Geplant wie ein Anbau an ein Sommerhaus, dient der kleine

The daily play of light and shade is essential for architecture and nature alike. This, and the slow changing of the seasons and the constant surprises provided by the weather present us an opportunity to create architecture that expresses time, the fourth dimension.

Winter adds a touch of its own to the Finnish landscape, altering the features of both buildings and landscapes under a blanket of white. Moreover, the weight caused by snow when it melts also has to be taken into consideration, resulting in heavier constructions than in more southerly climes. Snow is certainly an aesthetic blessing, transforming the scenery in a magical way. This phenomenon is a wonderful opportunity for both architecture and landscape design, but regrettably is seldom exploited.

Of the three little temples of enjoyment presented here, two are situated on the edge of Helsinki, and one in virgin nature. All three tackle the problem of serving a specific human activ-

Von der Aussichtsplattform eröffnet sich ein atemberaubender Blick auf die Stadt. Das Holzgitter gewährt den nötigen Durchblick und gibt dem Bau die erforderliche Festigkeit bei geringem Gewicht.

The lookout tower provides a breathtaking view of the city. The wooden latticework lends the lightweight structure the necessary strength while providing plenty of opportunity for viewing the surroundings.

Zufluchtsort der Bewunderung der Natur. Das lichtdurchflutete Innere bietet eine Reihe sorgfältig inszenierter Blicke zum Horizont, zum Himmel und hügelabwärts. Die Innenausstattung ist sehr raffiniert, eigentlich etwas fremd im ländlichen finnischen Kontext. Das Äußere sucht mit der Umgebung zu harmonieren, indem es das Erscheinungsbild eines großen grauen Steinblocks annimmt. Bei dieser Camouflage wird Ehrlichkeit gepflegt durch die Verwendung strikter geometrischer Formen. Der gekippte Würfel berührt das Gelände so leicht wie möglich und verweist so auf die bloß temporäre Präsenz des Menschen in der ewigen Natur.

Schutz für Schachspieler. Der symmetrische Bau dient als Basis für Schachspieler im Freien. Er steht auf der zentralen Achse einer kleinmaßstäblichen Parkkomposition am Rande des großen historischen Parkareals Kaivopuisto. Der ehrwürdige historische Park liegt an der südlichsten Spitze der Helsinki-Halbinsel, auf drei Seiten von der See umgeben. Der Pavillon dient als offenes Gemeinschaftshaus für den Schachverein im Park. Er bietet Schutz vor Regen und die vorherrschenden Südwestwinde. Einerseits soll der Status eines öffentlichen Gebäudes erkennbar sein, andererseits

ity while trying to merge in with their surroundings. None of the three follow models set by tradition, but rely on the influences of the site.

Lookout tower. This exciting structure sits on top of a prominent bedrock promontory on the western edge of Korkeasaari, Helsinki's zoo island. The innovative wooden construction is simultaneously transparent and volume-forming. The grid refers to the caged-in animals of a zoo, while the bubble shape of the structure resembles an eye – a suitable symbol for a viewing platform. The contrast between the heavy rock base and the airy lightweight structure creates visual tension. The fresh brownish colour of the wood will turn grey with the passing of time, blending it in with the colour of the concrete base, and that of the frequently-clouded sky.

Despite the conspicuous siting, which was necessary in view of the function of the tower, the building fits in with its surroundings thanks to its organic shape. Unfortunately, the ground-level arrangements are not as convincing as the overall concept. The vague stone curb stands in contrast to the clarity of the tower, strangling its optimism with conventional stuffiness. A simpler approach would have been more conducive to the integrity of the whole design.

Pleasure cabin. The tiny hut – an annex to a summer villa – is situated in an area of seemingly untouched nature, in an archetypal Finnish landscape of lakes and forests. The site is a rocky hill with sparse vegetation and spindly pine-trees. The small retreat focuses on enabling admiration of nature from within the confines of a room. The light-flushed interior provides a variety of carefully controlled views of the horizon, the sky and the downhill landscape.

Auf einen flechten-bewachsenen Felsen im finnischen Mäntyharju stellte der Architekt Juhani Pallasmaa 2002 ein winziges Häuschen. Die Glasfront öffnet den schräggestellten Holzkubus zum Himmel sowie zum Kallavesi-See.

In 2002, the architect Juhani Pallasmaa placed a tiny hut onto a lichen-covered rock in Mäntyharju, Finland. The glass front of the backwards-tilted wooden cube opens it up to the sky and to views of Lake Kallavesi far below.

Der graue Würfel fügt sich harmonisch in die finnische Landschaft um den Kallavesi-See und erinnert an einen Felsblock. Durch die klare geometrische Form wird dieses Bild jedoch nicht überstrapaziert.

The exterior of the grey cube harmonises with the environment by taking on the appearance of a large grey boulder. Honesty is maintained in this camouflage with the use of clear, geometrical forms.

versucht der Bau den Einfluss auf das Areal zu minimieren. Ein dünner Stahlrahmen und die reichliche Verwendung von Glas für die Außenwände ermöglichen den ungehinderten Blick vom Park zum Meer. Das flügelähnliche Dach, getragen von einer leichten Konstruktion, scheint zu schweben. Die horizontalen Stahlrohre unterstreichen die Weite des Meeres im Hintergrund. Manche Betrachter mögen sich am ausgeprägten modernistischen Aussehen stoßen, aber der öffentliche Charakter des Pavillons verlangte ein starkes Zeichen.

Diese funktional und architektonisch unterschiedlichen Beispiele teilen zumindest eine gemeinsame Qualität: Sie erfassen den Ort und beweisen, dass eins plus eins drei sein kann.

The interior is extremely refined, creating a slightly alienating effect in the rural Finnish context. The exterior seeks to harmonise with the environment by taking on the appearance of a large grey boulder, whereby honesty is maintained in the camouflage with the use of strictly geometrical, man-made forms. The tilted cube touches the site as lightly as possible, implying the temporary nature of man's presence in the permanence of nature.

Chess players' shelter. The symmetrical structure – a base for outdoor chess players – is set on the central axis of a small-scale park composition within Kaivopuisto park. The venerable historical park covers the southernmost tip of the Helsinki peninsula, and is bordered on three sides by the sea. The shelter serves as a kind of open community building for the park chess club, providing protection from rain and the prevailing south-westerly winds. While acknowledging its status as a public building, the shelter attempts to minimise its impact on the site. An unhindered view of the sea is ensured by the thin steel framework and the abundant use of glass walls.

The individualistic V-shaped roof is set floating by the lightweight understructure, while the horizontal steel tubes underline the infinity of the sea in the background. It is possible that some people do not like the modernist look, but the public nature of the shelter justifies a powerful presence.

These functionally and architecturally varied examples share at least one thing in common: they take the character of their surroundings into consideration while proving that one and one can indeed equal three.

Klangturm in Souru, Finnland

Souru Sound Tower, Finland

Souru is located in a beautiful lake area in eastern Finland, close to the town of Kuopio, and was once a village. Its foundations go back to 1868, when several iron mills were gaining their raw material from the bottom of the lake. Souru grew up around a huge factory building equipped with a steam engine, a steam hammer and a tall chimney. The village only existed for 40 years, from 1868 to 1908, but nevertheless had named streets, street lighting with gas lamps and a small hospital, and a population of some 600 in its best days. The village school and houses for the workers were located a mere 200 meters or so from the factory, and fields were situated nearby, but life in Souru was not easy as it involved twelve-hour work shifts and no meal breaks. Be that as it may, some 2,000 people spent most of their lives within its confines. In 1905, fire destroyed the workers' houses, and the decline of Souru began.

Now, almost 100 years later, it is a fascinating place to visit. It has basically reverted to forest, with pine trees, spruces and birches covering the whole area. Most of the buildings were demolished after the Second World War, and the materials used elsewhere. The only thing that still stands proudly is the factory chimney. The Finnish Board of Antiquities started to study the possibilities of preserving the site a few years ago, clearing undergrowth away from the old streets and the place where the factory once stood to reveal the old foundations of almost every building. Apart from these efforts, the forest was left untouched, preserving its atmosphere.

We were asked by the Board to come up with ideas on how to make the former village an interesting place to visit. Visiting the site was fascinating as one could sense the traces of people as if

Souru liegt in Ostfinnland, in der Nähe der Stadt Kuopio. Die Siedlung und das Eisenwerk wurden 1868 in einer wundervollen Seenlandschaft gegründet. Zu dieser Zeit gab es mehrere Eisenfabriken in Finnland. Das Rohmaterial bezogen sie vom Grunde der Seen. Herz der Produktion in Souro war ein riesiges Fabrikgebäude mit einer Dampfmaschine, einem Dampfhammer und einem hohen Kamin. Souru existierte nur 40 Jahre, von 1868 bis 1908. In seinen besten Tagen lebten rund 600 Menschen dort. Der Ort besaß sogar Straßennamen, Straßenbeleuchtung mit Gaslaternen und ein eigenes kleines Krankenhaus. Die Häuser der Arbeiter und die Dorfschule standen nur rund 200 Meter von der Fabrik entfernt. In der Nähe der Häuser fanden sich Felder. Das Leben in Souru war hart, mit Zwölf-Stunden-Schichten ohne Essenspausen. Aber trotzdem verbrachten etwa 2 000 Menschen ihr ganzes Leben dort. 1905 zerstörte Feuer die Wohngebäude und der Niedergang der Siedlung begann.

Es ist faszinierend, diesen Ort nach 100 Jahren zu besuchen. Im Grunde besteht er heute aus Wald. Kiefern, Fichten und Birken bedecken das ganze Gebiet. Ein Großteil der Gebäude wurde abgerissen, die Materialien anderenorts für den Wiederaufbau nach dem Zweiten Weltkrieg verwendet. Entlang der Forststraßen kann man zwar noch immer die Fundamente von fast allen Gebäuden finden, aber einzig der Fabrikschlot steht noch. Vor einigen Jahren begann das finnische Zentralamt für

Vesa Honkonen

Ein hölzerner Turm mit einer Klanginstallation erinnert an eine ehemalige Arbeitersiedlung mitten im Wald.

A wooden tower equipped with a sound installation recalls a former workers' village in the midst of a forest.

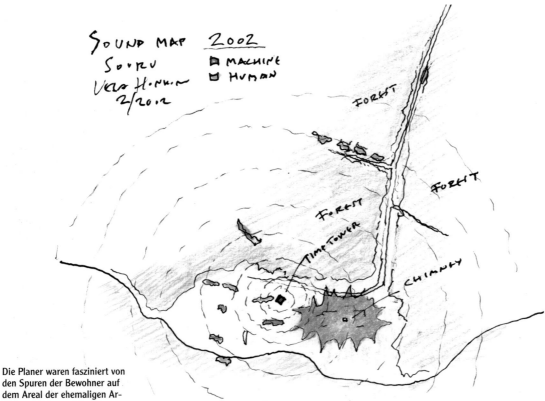

SOUND MAP 2002
SOVRV
VELS HINKIN
2/2012

☐ MACHINE
☐ HUMAN

FOREST
FOREST
FOREST
TIME TOWER
CHIMNEY

they were still around. We could almost hear the steam hammer, the children running to school and fishermen returning from the lake. This gave us the idea to recreate the place with sounds and recall the past with written artifacts and old photographs. In other words, to create an architecture that addresses the senses.

Since the best way to present the sounds was to use a Dolby surround system, we needed a place to house the loudspeakers, a shelter or structure that would enable visitors to experience the sounds and observe the area. Our solution was to create a tower, a time tower. In terms of design, we wanted its form language to distin-

Die Planer waren fasziniert von den Spuren der Bewohner auf dem Areal der ehemaligen Arbeitersiedlung und des Eisenwerks. In Gedanken hörten sie den Fabrikslärm und die Geräusche des Alltags. Sie skizzierten eine mögliche Geräuschkulisse (oben). Für den Aussichtsturm verwendeten sie finnische Kiefer, geschützt durch einen Teer-Anstrich. Einziger Zeuge der Vergangenheit ist der Fabrikschlot.

The planners were fascinated by the traces of the workers who had once lived around the iron mill. Walking through the forest, they felt they could hear the racket of the factory and the noises of everyday life, and this gave them the idea of recreating the place with sounds (see sketch above). Rough Finnish pine provided with a tar finish has been used to create the time tower. The only artefact of the past is the factory chimney.

Die asymmetrische Form des Turms ergibt sich aus akustischen Überlegungen. Die vertikale Struktur der Holzkonstruktion nimmt den Rhythmus des Kiefernforsts auf. Sobald Besucher den Aussichtsturm betreten, erinnert die Toninstallation an den früheren Alltag. Außer einem Überblick über das Gebiet bietet die obere Etage eine Sammlung historischer Pläne und Photos.

The wooden tower was given an asymmetrical shape for acoustic reasons, and its vertical forms take up the rhythm of the pine forest. The moment the tower is entered, a sound recording will recall everyday life as it was once lived at the workers settlement. A map of the area and historic plans and photographs are to be displayed on the upper level.

Souru Sound Tower, Finland
Client: National Board of Antiquities; Kari Nikkanen, Päivi Eronen
Architect: Vesa Honkonen, Vesa Honkonen Architects
Collaborators: Mari Koskinen, Ulla Kuitunen, Oliver Walter, Mikolaj Smolenski
Sound design: Vesa Honkonen & Juha Westman
Sound: Juha Westman
Structural engineer: Juhani Väisänen, Insinööritoimisto Juhani Väisänen Ky
Construction: 2002
The sound tower will be opened in spring 2003.

Museen und Denkmalpflege die Möglichkeiten auszuloten, die Reste des Ortes zu erhalten. Der Bewuchs auf den alten Straßen und dem Ort, wo die Fabrik stand, wurde gerodet, die Fundamente und Strukturen freigelegt. Andererseits konnte auch der Wald und seine Atmosphäre bewahrt werden. Das Amt beauftragte unser Büro, Überlegungen anzustellen, die Siedlungen interessant für Besucher zu machen. Es war faszinierend, durch den Wald zu spazieren und die Spuren der ehemaligen Bewohner zu finden: Man konnte beinahe die Dampfhämmer hören, die Kinder, die zur Schule rennen, und die Fischer, die vom See kommen. Dies gab uns die Idee für eine Architektur, die alle Sinne anspricht. Warum sollten wir nicht der Geschichte lauschen, den Ort in unseren Gedanken mit Tönen, Geräuschen, der geschriebenen Geschichte und mit alten Fotografien wieder erschaffen?

Es brauchte eine schützende Konstruktion, um Klänge und Geräusche der Vergangenheit mit einem Dolby-Surround-System zu präsentieren. Dieser Bau sollte gleichzeitig Besuchern die Möglichkeit bieten, das Areal zu betrachten. Die Lösung war ein Turm, ein Zeit-Turm. Der Bau benötigte einen klaren Ortsbezug, ohne jedoch an historische Gebäude zu erinnern. Deshalb wählten wir als Material raues finnisches Holz, Kiefer mit einem Teer-Anstrich. Die Struktur musste vor Ort gebaut werden. Das gab einige Anforderungen für die Details vor, die aus diesem Grund etwas derb erscheinen. Der Turm sollte nicht so klar die Richtung und Beziehungen zu den Ruinen aufnehmen, die Struktur spielt auch mit dem Rhythmus des Kiefernforsts. Beide Elemente beeinflussten den Entwurf.

Die Geräusche sollen sich im Turm »bewegen«, Klang generiert also die runde asymmetrische Form im Grundriss. Die Dynamik der gekrümmten Wände setzt sich nach oben fort, die Wände lehnen sich in den Kurven nach außen. Das Spiel von Licht und Schatten enthüllt die Ästhetik dieser dynamischen Form. Schlitze in den Wänden lassen diese halbtransparent wirken und ermöglichen Blicke auf die Umgebung. Die Holzlatten werden durch kleine Holzblöcke zusammengehalten, die einem zufälligen Rhythmus folgen. Der Geruch des Teers weckt die Sinne.

Menschen werden nach Souru kommen, den Turm sehen, betreten und dann beginnt die Geschichte zu sprechen. Die Klangwelt startet automatisch, wenn Besucher hochklettern. In der oberen Etage des Turms werden Landkarten und Fotos präsentiert. Der Turm selbst ist ein Denkmal für die Menschen, die einst dort lebten und arbeiteten. Für zehn Minuten wird ihre Geschichte wieder zum Leben erweckt.

guish it from the traces of the past yet create a relationship to both the place and life as it was once lived in the village. For this reason, we chose rough Finnish pine with a tar finish as the main material. Moreover, the structure had to be capable of being built on site, requiring a fair degree of detailing and being the reason for a certain roughness. As we did not want it to point too clearly to the ruins or stand in visible relationship to them, the wooden tower also takes up the rhythm of the pine forest. Both elements influenced the design.

Since we wanted the sounds to seem to move around inside the tower, an asymmetric circular ground plan was the result. The curve of the walls becomes stronger the higher they get, with the result that they start to lean out as if succumbing to centrifugal forces. The aesthetics of these shapes will become more apparent when the tower is seen in the play of light and shade. Slits in the walls make them semi-transparent and provide views of the surroundings, and are achieved by using wooden slats randomly held together by small wooden blocks. The scent of tar addresses the senses.

People coming to Souru will see the tower, and the moment they enter it history will start to speak, recreated by a sound recording that automatically starts when visitors climb up to the entrance. Old maps and photographs will be displayed on the upper level of the tower, which in itself is a monument to the people who lived in Souru in 1868 and 1908, as commemorated on a cast iron plate. For ten minutes these people will come alive again. And when the visitors leave, the tower will go back to being part of the forest and landscape.

Rastplätze am Oslofjord

Rest stops at Oslofjord

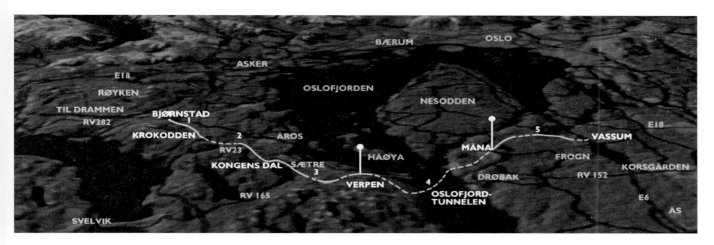

More and more highways are being added to the road network in Norway, including a new link that has been built south of Oslo between the E18 and the E6. Crossing the Oslofjord, it leads through a varied landscape of fields and deciduous and coniferous woods, providing stunning views of the fjord below. At the plan approval phase in 1995, high aesthetic quality was made one of the objectives of the project in view of the spectacular landscape the road passes through.

This approach also applied to the design of the rest stops, which had to take both nature and civil engineering into consideration. A landscape architect was especially detailed to the project by the Norwegian highway authorities to ensure that the road fits in with its surroundings. One of the first things she did was draw up aesthetic guidelines for the authorities, sub-contractors etc. involved in the project. Her requirements included consideration of the proximity of the fjord and countryside in the design

Norwegens Straßennetz wird immer dichter. Eine neue Strecke verbindet südlich von Oslo die E18 mit der E6 und unterquert dabei den Oslofjord. Die Straße führt durch eine abwechslungsreiche Landschaft mit Feldern, Laub- und Nadelwäldern sowie mit wunderbarer Aussicht auf den Fjord. Deshalb wurde schon bei der Planfeststellung 1995 eine hohe ästhetische Qualität angestrebt, was sich schließlich auch in der Gestaltung von Rastplätzen niederschlug, die zwischen der Kulturlandschaft und dem technischen Bauwerk vermitteln. Um die landschaftliche Einbindung zu gewährleisten, stellte das Norwegische Straßenbauamt eine Landschaftsarchitektin für dieses Projekt ab, die zunächst für die Vielzahl der am Bau Beteiligten ästhetische Leitlinien festlegte. Ausgewogen sollte in der Gestaltung der Elemente sowohl die Fjordnähe wie auch die Waldlandschaft berücksichtigt werden. Stein und Holz sollten als Materialien vorherrschen.

Zwei Rastplätze gibt es, inmitten interessanter Pflanzen- und Geländeformationen. Da man hier dem Verkehrsprojekt am nächsten kommt, wurde auf Gestaltung und Ausführung besonderes Gewicht gelegt: Künstler, Industriedesigner, Architekt und Landschaftsarchitekten haben dabei eng zusammengearbeitet. Der Kontrast zwischen dem Auto als technologischem Produkt und der Natur sollte bei den Elementen der Rastplätze

Kirstine Laukli
Erik Wessel

Elemente der Wald- und Fjordlandschaft spiegeln sich in den Materialien von Möbeln und kleinen Bauten der Rastplätze wider.

Materials that refer to the nearby forests and fjords have been used for the furniture items, viewing towers and other structures.

Eine neue Straße im Großraum Oslo verbindet zwei wichtige Routen und unterquert dabei den Oslofjord in einem Tunnel. Aufgrund der Nähe zum Fjord und der abwechslungsreichen Landschaft legten die Planer hohen Wert auf landschaftliche Einbindung.

A new road in the greater Oslo region links two important motorways, passing below Oslofjord through a subsea tunnel. Due to the spectacular landscape and proximity of the fjord, the planners took care to ensure that the road fits in with its surroundings.

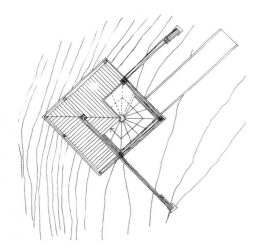

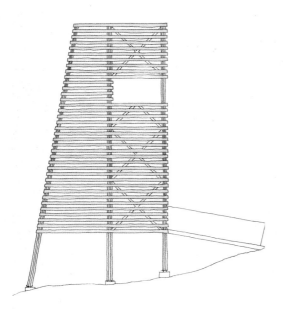

of rest stop elements, and use of wood and stone as the main materials.

The landscape architect chose to locate the two rest stops involved in the project in an area characterised by interesting vegetation, topographical formations, and interesting views. Since the rest stops are close to the road, particular attention was paid to the design and execution aspects involved, entailing close collaboration between the artist, industry designer, architect and landscape architect.

In the design of the site furniture, viewing towers and so on, the objective was to underscore the contrast of nature and technology, as demonstrated in car advertisements, which are generally set in the countryside and rarely in the sort of surroundings where cars are usually encountered.

The rest stops are located high above the Oslofjord, and offer breathtaking views. Accordingly, the objective was to provide a graduated hierarchy in formal design terms to enable enjoyment of the scenery on the one hand, and a sense of intimacy at the places set aside for people to eat, drink and talk on the other. Provision of space for games and movement was another objective.

To cover all the spatial aspects, the furniture groups are of differing character in terms of compactness. At the car park and the vantage points, the units placed along the stone wall that marks off the car park feature an awning to create a feeling of intimacy but not provide shelter from rain, which would be fairly senseless in a country where it mainly comes down at an almost flat angle. The awnings create a maritime, sail-like effect in reference to the fjord, and are

Um ein einheitliches Erscheinungsbild der Rastplätze zu erreichen, verwendeten die Planer Holzlamellen für die unterschiedlichen Elemente wie Hocker, Bänke, Tische, Dächer, Klohäuser und Aussichtstürme. Steinmauern grenzen die Sitzplätze vom Parkplatz ab.

In order to create a uniform look for the rest stops, the designers used slatted planking for the various elements, such as stools, benches, tables, toilet buildings and lookout towers. Stone wall separate the seating units from the car park.

Elegante hölzerne Aussichtstürme ragen zwischen den
Baumwipfeln hoch und ma-
chen schon von weitem auf die
Rastplätze aufmerksam.

Elegant wooden lookout
towers emerge from among
the treetops, thus drawing
attention to the rest stops
from afar.

eine Rolle spielen, ähnlich wie in der Werbung für neue Automodelle, die immer mit einer Naturszenerie als Hintergrund vorgestellt werden.

Die Rastplätze liegen erhöht, mit Aussicht über den großen Landschaftsraum Oslofjord. Ziel war es, den Kontakt zur Landschaft herzustellen und dennoch eine intime Stimmung zu schaffen, wo sich die Menschen an einen Tisch setzen und kommunizieren. Um all die räumlichen Aufgaben zu lösen, wählten wir eine unterschiedliche Anordnung der Möbelgruppen. In der Nähe des Parkplatzes, an den Aussichtspunkten, platzierten wir die Möbel an einer Steinmauer, die zugleich die räumliche Grenze zum Parkplatz markiert. Ein Dach soll ein Gefühl des Geborgenseins vermitteln. Es ist nicht als Schutz vor dem Regen gedacht, was ja auch ziemlich unnütz wäre in einem Land, in dem der Regen meist horizontal daherkommt. Zudem sollte es maritim wirken, um die Nähe zum Fjord zu unterstreichen. Man könnte das Dach mit einem Segel assoziieren, bestehend aus durchsichtig-weißem Polykarbonat. Von den Bäumen fallende Blätter sind von unten sichtbar und schaffen interessante visuelle Variationen.

Die Möbel an den Aussichtspunkten sind rechteckig geformt und fächerförmig angeordnet, mit der kurzen Seite zur Aussicht. Die anderen Sitzmöbel, im Gelände verteilt, sind quadratisch, ohne Dach. Laubbäume und Kiefern bilden die Baumvegetation, was einen leichten Eindruck ergibt durch die nicht zu dicken Stämme. Dazu passend wurde das Material gewählt, wir konstruierten Möbel mit dünnen Lamellen-Stäben. Um ein technisches Aussehen zu erreichen, wie es zum Charakter des Ortes passt, wählten wir säurefesten Stahl für die Untergestelle, die somit verrottungsfrei Hocker und Tische fest verankern, selbst mit nur einem Ankerpunkt.

Die Aussichtstürme sind die spektakulärsten Elemente der Rastplätze. Sie bieten formidable Weitblicke und scheinen mit den Antennen im Landschaftsraum zu korrespondieren. Auch die Türme sind maritim ausgeprägt, denn ihre Form ist von den Baken abgeleitet, die überall an der norwegischen Küste zu finden sind. Eine ähnliche Formensprache wurde bei den Toilettengebäuden angewandt. Sie sind einfache Satteldachhäuser mit einer robusten Bretterverkleidung aus sibirischer Lärche in einem Muster, das man auch in Möbeln, Baldachinen, Türmen und Holzbrücken entlang der Wege wiedersieht. Das Dach ist mit patiniertem Zinkblech gedeckt, ein Material, das im Aussehen nah an den Stahl herankommt, der sonst verwendet wurde. Ein Säulengang am Funktionsgebäude bietet einen schützenden Unterstand.

Rest stops at Oslofjord Highway, Norway
Client: Statens vegvesen, Buskerud
Responsible landscape architect on the project: Kirstine Laukli
Landscape planning, rest stops: Hindhamar a.s., Åse Skrøvseth, landscape architect
Furniture and viewing platform design: Erik Wessel, artist, and Ivar Grødal, industrial designer
Toilet building design: Finn Solli, Sivilarkitekt
Planning: 1997 – 1999
Construction: 1999 – 2000

made of semi-transparent white polycarbonate fabric that makes it possible to see fallen leaves from below in interesting variations.

The furniture at the vantage points is rectangular in shape and positioned in fan-like arrangements that face onto the view. The other seating items, which are scattered throughout the site, are square in shape and do not have awnings. Existing pines and deciduous species with slender trunks acted as the inspiration in creating furniture with a light and airy effect. Use has been made of acid-proof steel for the supporting structures of the furniture to introduce a technical touch befitting the character of a place close to the road. This has the additional advantage that the supports will not rot or become loose, despite having only one anchor point.

The viewing towers are the most spectacular elements of the rest stops. Providing views of the whole landscape, they are inspired by the beacons found all along the Norwegian coast, and while being maritime in character, seem to correspond with the antennas dotted around the countryside.

A similar form idiom is evident in the toilet building provided at each rest stop. These buildings consist of simple saddleback-roofed structures. The walls are made of planks in Siberian larch, and create the slatted effect that is also encountered in the furniture, awnings and towers and the wooden bridges along the paths. A covered walkway flanks the buildings on two sides to provide protection from the weather, and the roofs are covered in pre-patinated zinc sheeting, a material that resembles the steel used in the other elements.

In 2001, the whole project gained the Global Road Achievement Award in the Design and Construction Methodology categories (in the latter area for the freezing technology used to stabilize a zone of loose deposits in a subsea tunnel).

Bäume, Hütten, Wartehäuschen

Trees, huts, shelters

The Sheltered Tree. About ten years ago there was just one project that occupied my mind: The Sheltered Tree. My idea was to find a place as un-inviting as possible, to plant a tree there and protect it in a greenhouse. This installation, a kind of incubator, that provides the optimum climate for the tree, was for me a picture of our paradox need to choose something from the broad mass and protect it by every possible means, thus for instance like landscaping a garden and creating "little paradises" there.

Involved here is a schematic landscaping structure containing the archetype "house" and the archetype "tree" in the reverse relation. It is not the tree that does the protecting, but vice versa. One could also view the tree as an individual, a living being comparable with a human being, offering the possibility of identification.

I found that Iceland would be the best place for an installation of this kind. There is enough energy there to operate a greenhouse and the Icelanders are, as is generally known, continually occupied with planting trees. However, trees growing outside were, to the general displeasure of all, only planted as fodder for freely roaming sheep. A tree "under glass", so I thought, could be a solution.

Since practically the entire population of Iceland lives in Reykjavik or in the direct vicinity, I came to the conclusion that the road between the town and the airport would be a strategically good place. The route is bordered by desolate fields of lava that would offer a sufficiently contrasting background. Of course, the greenhouse should also be illuminated in the darkness of winter. I saw before me an illuminated, slender but tall greenhouse with a blossoming orange

Der Geschützte Baum. Vor etwa zehn Jahren beschäftigte mich nur ein Projekt: Der Geschützte Baum. Meine Idee war, einen Platz zu finden, so ungastlich wie möglich, dort einen Baum zu pflanzen und diesen mit einem Gewächshaus zu schützen. Diese Installation, eine Art Brutkasten, der das optimale Klima für den Baum schafft, war für mich ein Bild unseres paradoxen Bedürfnisses, etwas aus der breiten Masse auszuwählen und dieses mit allen Mitteln zu schützen, also zum Beispiel Gärten anzulegen und dort kleine Paradiese zu schaffen. Es handelt sich um eine schematische Landschaftsgestaltung, die den Archetyp »Haus« und den Archetyp »Baum« in umgekehrtem Verhältnis enthält. Es ist nicht der Baum, der schützt, sondern umgekehrt. Man könnte den Baum auch als ein Individuum betrachten, ein Lebewesen vergleichbar dem Menschen, die Möglichkeit der Identifizierung bietend.

Ich fand, Island müsste der beste Platz für eine solche Installation sein. Dort gibt es genug Energie, um ein Gewächshaus zu betreiben, und die Isländer sind, wie allgemein bekannt, ständig damit beschäftigt, Bäume zu pflanzen. Im Freien wachsende Bäume wurden allerdings, zum allgemeinen Verdruss, bisher nur zu Futter für die frei laufenden Schafe. Der »eingeglaste Baum«, dachte ich, könnte eine Lösung sein. Da nahezu die gesamte Bevölkerung Islands in Reykjavik oder in unmittelbarer Nähe dazu wohnt, kam ich zu der Auffassung, dass die Straße zwischen der Stadt und dem Flugplatz eine strategisch gute Lage bot. Der Weg ist eingerahmt von trostlosen Lavafeldern, die einen hinreichend kontrastierenden Hintergrund bieten würden. Natürlich sollte das Gewächshaus auch in der Dunkelheit des Winters leuchten. Ich sah vor mir ein leuchtendes, schmales aber hohes Glashaus mit einem beleuchteten, blühenden Orangenbaum darin. Es war wohl das Paradoxe und Surrealistische an diesem Bild, das mich antrieb. Beinahe gelang es mir, den Geschäftsführer der Aluminiumhütte in Hafnarfjordur bei Reykjavik, zum Sponsoring des gesamten Projektes zu bewegen. Aber als wir nähere Einzelheiten

Monika Gora

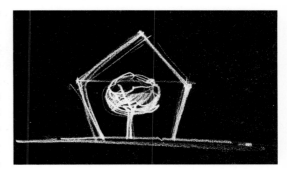

Menschen suchen Schutz, im Garten wie in der Landschaft. Aber der ideale Unterschlupf muss auch Ausblick gewähren.

People seek shelter in the garden just as in the countryside. But the ideal place to seek shelter must allow a view outside.

Das Projekt »Der geschützte Baum« kehrt das Verhältnis der Archetypen Baum und Haus um. Ein Glashaus an einem möglichst ungastlichen Ort sollte als schützender Brutkasten für einen Baum dienen. Die Umsetzung in Island scheiterte am Sponsor.

The project "Sheltered Tree" reverses the relation of the archetypes tree and house. A greenhouse in a highly uninviting place was to serve as a protective incubator for a tree. The realization of the concept in Iceland failed on account of the sponsor.

tree lit up inside. It must have been the paradoxical and surrealistic aspect of this picture that drove me on.

I almost managed to persuade the manager of the aluminium foundry in Hafnarfjordur, near Reykjavik to sponsor the entire project. But when we discussed this in further detail, the double meaning behind this project dawned on him. Protection requires a need for protection; that is to say, it also needs something one has to protect oneself against. If one then comes along with a tree that is so securely packed, one could assume with some distrust, that environmental problems could exist here that are perhaps even caused by the aluminium factory itself. And of course I could not dispute this interpretation; in fact I even thought that this was a good, ambivalence that sets one thinking.

Shelters, Castles in the Air. By the term "shelter" one mostly means, as I have said, protection for people and not for trees. One thinks of a roof over one's head and of houses. In environmental psychology the term "prospect refuge" exists, a useful mixture of view and protection, according to definition this is on a small elevation, protected by treetops – a place from where one can glance out into the open. We give preference to places of this kind due to our past as hunters in the savannah.

Due to my scepticism I arrived at another, perhaps more relevant explanation. Surrounding oneself by enveloping elements arouses a feeling of comfort and security. This can be a hug, a blanket, a chair, a telephone booth, a bus stop shelter, a pergola, a veranda. To envelope oneself is a possibility for making a place one's own. A place, shut off from the rest of the world.

diskutierten, kam er hinter die doppelte Bedeutung des Projektes. Schutz setzt ein Bedürfnis nach Schutz voraus, also auch etwas, vor dem man sich schützen muss. Kommt man nun mit einem so sicher eingepackten Baum daher, könnte man mit einigem Misstrauen annehmen, dass hier Umweltprobleme existieren, vielleicht sogar durch das Aluminiumwerk selbst verursacht. Und natürlich konnte ich dieser Auslegung nicht widersprechen, vielmehr dachte ich, dass diese für sich eine gute und gedankenweckende Zweideutigkeit war.

Hütten, Luftschlösser. Mit dem Begriff »shelter« meint man, wie gesagt, meist Schutz für Menschen, nicht für Bäume. Man denkt an ein Dach über dem Kopf und an Häuser. In der Umweltpsychologie gibt es den Begriff »prospect refuge«, eine zweckmäßige Mischung aus Aussicht und Schutz, laut Definition auf einer kleinen Anhöhe, von Baumkronen geschützt – ein Platz, von dem man auf das offene Gelände blicken kann. Solche Plätze bevorzugen wir aufgrund unserer Vergangenheit als Jäger in der Savanne.

At the housing exhibition Bo01 in Malmö one and a half years ago, the whole area of an exhibition park was laid out with an "energy" forest, i.e. with salix (osier and sallow) – dense and in some places, an extensively cultivated thicket. There, children had built little huts out of left-over building materials in a project initiated by some schoolteachers. At the beginning the children were given help in erecting them; later the project ran on its own. Soon there were several hundred small huts, little places for sheltering under, scattered throughout the thicket. A wealth of spontaneous innovative spirit and creativity which was completely overlooked by the organisers, perhaps also because it was difficult to find a

In meiner Skepsis kam ich zu einer anderen, vielleicht näherliegenden Erklärung. Sich mit umschließenden Elementen zu umgeben, gibt ein Gefühl der Geborgenheit. Das kann eine Umarmung sein, eine Decke, ein Sessel, eine Telefonzelle, ein Wartehäuschen, eine Pergola, eine Veranda. Sich zu umschließen, ist eine Möglichkeit, einen Platz zu seinem Eigen zu machen. Ein Platz abgeschirmt vom Rest der Welt.

Auf der Wohnausstellung Bo01 in Malmö vor anderthalb Jahren gestaltete man die Fläche des Ausstellungsparks mit Energiewald, mit Salix (Korb- und Salweide) – dichte, und an manchen Stellen ausgedehnte Anpflanzungen voller Gestrüpp. Dort hatten Kinder in einem von Kinderpädagogen initiierten Projekt Reste von Baumaterialien zu kleinen Hütten verbaut. Bekamen die Kinder anfangs Hilfe bei der Errichtung, so lief das Projekt später von alleine. Bald waren mehrere hundert kleine Hütten, kleine Unterschlupfe, im dichten Gestrüpp verstreut. Eine Ansammlung von spontanem Erfindungsreichtum und Kreativität, der von den Organisato-

An Storchennester erinnern die Luftschlösser genannten Aussichtswarten (links). Gebaut wurden die Nester aus Stroh für die Bo01 in Malmö.
Die Strandkörbe auf der grünen Wiese eines Altersheimes in Falun verlocken zum Besuch des Gartens.

The observation points are called "Castles in the Air" (left) – their appearance reminding one of storks' nests. The nests for the Bo01 in Malmö were made of straw.
"Garden Settlers" next to an old people's home in Falun entice people to visit the garden.

ren völlig übersehen wurde, vielleicht auch weil es schwer war, eine Klassifizierung dafür zu finden. In der Presse wurde nicht ein einziges Wort über die Hütten verloren und kaum einer der Besucher hat sie gesehen. Schade, denn sie waren Ausdruck eines grundlegenden, räumlichen Bedürfnisses und interessant anzusehen.

Ich selbst hatte im Rahmen dieser Ausstellung, gleich in der Nähe der wilden Hüttchenansammlung, ein Projekt mit Luftschlössern – ebenfalls sehr intime Bauwerke. Vom Aussehen her erinnerten sie an Vogelnester auf Hochspannungsmasten. Mit Wänden aus Stroh und ohne Dach waren sie auf Stützen aus Fachwerk in unterschiedlichen Höhen platziert, die niedrigen für die Vorsichtigen und die hohen für die Waghalsigen. Um in die höchsten klettern zu können, brauchte es Anstrengung und Mut. Belohnung war die Spannung beim Klettern, der Ausblick und die Abgeschiedenheit da oben im Nest.

Bewegung, Strandkörbe im Grünen, Buswartehäuschen. Die meisten erleben Landschaft heutzutage aus der schützenden Hülle ihres Autos heraus. Das abgeschirmte Innere erscheint wie eine Fortsetzung der häuslichen Geborgenheit, wie ein bequemes und umschließendes Möbel. Man betrachtet die Landschaft durch die Autoscheiben. In der »Prospect refuge«-Theorie ersetzt das Auto die Baumkronen und bietet beides, sichere Bequemlichkeit und Freiheit in der eigentlichen Bewegung durch die Landschaft. Ich spreche vom Auto, aber natürlich sind alle Fahrzeuge interessante kleine mobile Bauwerke.

Die »Garden Settlers« (Strandkörbe im Grünen) entstanden als imaginäre Fahrzeuge bei der Renovierung eines Altersheimes in Falun. Der Form nach erinnern sie an Strandkörbe oder an Bänke in Skiliften und alten Zugwaggons. Man denkt zurück an einen geschützten Sitzplatz mit aufregendem Ausblick. Ich dachte, dass gerade die Bewohner dieses Heimes aus ihrem Hochhaus hinaus gelockt werden mussten. Also konnten die Möbel zu Außenposten werden, Halteplätze, zu denen man schlendert, denkbare Treffpunkte. Die »Strandkörbe im Grünen« findet man direkt am Haus und auch etwas entfernt in der Nähe eines Flusses. Alle jedoch sind sie von den Fenstern des Heimes aus sichtbar. Der erzielte Effekt war größer als ich mir vorgestellt hatte. Wurde das Gelände vorher von keinem benutzt, so erwachte nun sogar das Interesse am Gärtnern. Die Rückseite des Hauses wurde in Ordnung gebracht und bepflanzt; das Personal begann einen Garten anzulegen und mit den Bewohnern hinauszugehen.

classification for it. Not one single word was mentioned in the press about the huts and hardly any of the visitors saw them. This was a pity, as they were an expression of a basic, spatial need and were interesting to look at.

I myself had a project with "Castles in the Air" at this exhibition, very close to the group of scattered huts – similarly very intimate constructions. Their appearance reminded one of birds' nests on high-voltage towers. With walls of straw and roofless, they were positioned on semi-timbered supports at different heights, the low ones for the cautious and the high ones for the more daring. Climbing up to the highest ones demanded a lot of effort and courage. This was rewarded by the excitement of climbing, the view and the remoteness up there in the nest.

Movement, Garden Settlers, bus stop shelters. Most people experience the countryside nowadays within the protective enclosure of their car. This shielded interior seems like a continuation of the domestic comfort and security, like a comfortable, enveloping piece of furniture. One looks at the countryside from the car window. The car replaces the treetops of the "prospect refuge" theory and offers both secure comfort and freedom in actually moving through the countryside. I mention the car, but of course all vehicles are interesting mobile structures.

The "Garden Settlers" came into being as imaginary vehicles in the course of renovating an old people's home in Falun. The form reminds one of beach basket seats or the benches on ski lifts and in old train compartments. One thinks back to a protected seat with a stimulating view. I thought that the residents of this home, especially, ought to be enticed out of their block of flats into the surrounding garden. The furniture could therefore become outposts, places to stop at that one strolls to, visual and practical fixed points, possible meeting places. The "Garden Settlers" are found directly next to the house and also a short distance away, near a river. However, they are all visible from the windows of the home. The effect obtained was greater than I had imagined. Whereas the surrounding garden had not been used by anyone beforehand, interest now even arose in gardening. The back of the house was tidied up and cultivated; the personnel began to landscape a garden and go outside with the residents.

Bus stop shelters are usually small and mostly completely nondescript constructions. They look trivial, mundane and weathered. In the hustle and bustle of the town they are noticed primarily because of their bright advertising posters, but otherwise they mostly blend into the townscape.

In the countryside the situation is quite different. There, the little bus stop grows to become a veritable terminal that assumes the same importance as the train station or airport elsewhere – a meeting point, a place for communication, a gateway to the outside world. A place where one begins or ends a journey, where one spends one's time, immersed in thought or conversing with other travellers. The bus stop shelter becomes an expression of our civilisation and actually gains a symbolic character for travellers and communication.

I had the possibility of developing two prototypes of bus stop shelters in rural areas, one for northern Sweden and one for the skerries near Stockholm. The architectural design of the bus

Buswartehäuschen sind gewöhnliche, kleine, meist völlig anonyme Bauwerke. Trivial, alltäglich und abgenutzt kommen sie daher. Im Trubel der Stadt fallen sie am ehesten durch ihre leuchtenden Reklameschilder auf und gehen ansonsten im Stadtbild meist unter. Ganz anders sieht es im ländlichen Raum aus. Dort wächst die kleine Haltestelle zu einem veritablen Terminal, das so wichtig ist wie anderswo der Bahnhof oder Flughafen: ein Treffpunkt, ein Ort der Kommunikation, ein Tor zur Welt. Ein Ort, an dem man eine Reise beginnt oder beendet, an dem man seine Zeit vertreibt, in Gedanken oder in Gespräche mit anderen Reisenden versunken. Das Wartehäuschen wird zu einem Ausdruck unserer Zivilisation und bekommt Symbolcharakter für die Reisenden und für Kommunikation an sich.

Ich bekam die Möglichkeit, zwei Prototypen für Buswartehäuschen im ländlichen Raum, einen für Nordschweden und einen für die Schären vor Stockholm, zu entwickeln. Die Häuschen passen sich in ihrer Architektur den Bautraditionen der entsprechenden Gegend an. Das gezimmerte in Nordschweden ist geformt wie eine gewölbte Handfläche, eine fünfeckige Form, die längste Seite den kommenden Bussen zugewendet. Im Inneren befindet sich eine gegen die Decke gerichtete indirekte Beleuchtung und der gebogenen Form folgende Sitzbänke. Das Wartehäuschen ist dafür konzipiert, einige Meter von der Straße entfernt zu stehen, sodass die Reisenden vor Schnee und Spritzern sicher sind. Eine zur Straße liegende Glasscheibe bietet sicheren Schutz vor Wind und vom Winterdienst zusammengeschobenen Schneebergen. Den »Typ Nord« gibt es in zwei verschiedenen Größen. Die Silhouette ist aus großer Entfernung wiedererkennbar. Alle verwendeten Materialien sind bodenständig, nutzen sich sehr langsam ab und altern in Würde: Holz, Zink und Naturfarbe, die zwar verblasst aber nicht abblättert. Da das ganze Bauwerk eine deutliche Formensprache und eine gediegene Bauweise aufweist, verträgt es auch eine Anhäufung von Schildern und Briefkästen, die die Zeit mit sich bringt. Kurzum, es wurde dafür entwickelt, Treffpunkt des kleinen Ortes zu werden.

Das zweite Wartehäuschen lehnt sich in seiner Ausführung an die leichte Sommerbauweise in den Schären vor Stockholm an. Es gleicht eher einer Veranda und ist aus Modulen zusammengesetzt, die in ihrer Größe und den Anteilen an Holz oder Glas variieren. Eine mögliche Weiterentwicklung des Projektes wäre eine Errichtung der Wartehäuschen an mehreren Stellen, sodass sie nach und nach zu Landmarken im Busverkehr der entsprechenden Regionen werden.

Die Buswartehäuschen orientieren sich an der Bautradition der entsprechenden Gegend. Das gezimmerte nordschwedische Modell (oben) besitzt eine fünfeckige Form. Die längste Seite ist den ankommenden Bussen zugewandt.
Das Wartehäuschen für die Schären vor Stockholm gleicht einer Veranda (unten).

The bus stop shelters comply with the building tradition of the respective region. The timbered model in northern Sweden (top) is a five-corned structure with the longest side facing the approaching busses. The bus stop shelter for the skerries near Stockholm resembles a veranda (bottom).

stops complies with the building tradition of the respective region.

The timbered one in northern Sweden is shaped like a cupped palm of a hand, a five-corned structure with the longest side facing the approaching busses. On the inside there is indirect lighting directed towards the roof and benches fitting the rounded shape. The bus stop shelter is designed so that the travellers can stand a few meters away from the road, thus protecting from snow and splashing. A glass pane facing the road provides reliable protection against the wind and the mounds of snow accumulating from the snowploughs. The "North Type" is available in two different sizes. The silhouette is clearly defined and pleasing to look at, and recognisable at a greater distance away. All the materials used are robust, wear very slowly and grow old in dignity, i.e. wood, zinc and natural paint that fades but does not peel off. Since the entire construction has a clear structural form and solid design, it also allows such additions as notices and letterboxes, as time goes by. In short, it was developed for becoming a meeting place in this small village.

The design of the second bus stop shelter is an imitation of the light summer architecture on the skerries near Stockholm. It is more like a veranda in modular construction, these modules varying in size and their proportions of wood or glass. A possible further development of the project would be to set up this bus stop shelter at several places, so that they gradually become landmarks for bus transport in the respective regions.

Umbrella-pergolas and rain fountain. Pergolas are constructions that substitute trees, linked with a home-like character. They offer gentle, airy, subtle protection; they hardly prevent rainwater from seeping through but they do provide protection against the sun and offer a certain feeling of solitude.

I presume that as good as all landscape architects experiment with differing types of pergolas as a supplement to outdoor greenery. For me personally, it is always exciting to try out the most differing forms and test the effects they are to achieve.

The last pergola I built is called "Parapluie" – umbrella. The French word *parapluie* literally means "protection against the rain", or to be exact, a shelter again, very close to the body, that at least provides some protection to the upper part and allows the possibility of free vision. My "Umbrella" protects the head from the rain and the artificial watering that starts up now and again while one's feet are being soaked in a misty spray. It is a grass hill on bronze legs that one can regard as a sort of organism or an unusual building covered with overgrowth.

The further development of the "Parapluie" is now leading to newly structures with overgrowth and on stilts. Pergolas as monuments in the countryside; fragments of undulating grass areas, fields or hills, resting on thin supports. Installations that wander across a town square, hovering together over the surface complementing each other. Small roofs that form lit up spaces at night or under which one simply finds protection. These new structures – like walking along a ridge between a building and a built-up landscape – will occupy a bordering zone in urban districts between grass areas and trees. They will intercommunicate with the treetops and draw them into the open countryside.

Regenschirm-Pergolen und Springbrunnen aus Regen. Pergolen sind konstruierte Substitute für Bäume, verbunden mit einer Anspielung auf ein Haus. Sie bieten zarten, luftigen, subtilen Schutz, der zwar Regenwasser kaum am Passieren hindert, aber der Schutz vor Sonnenstrahlen und eine gewisse Abgeschiedenheit bietet.

Ich nehme an, dass so gut wie alle Landschaftsarchitekten mit unterschiedlichen Typen von Pergolen als Ergänzung zu den sich frei entwickelnden Gewächsen experimentieren. Für mich selbst ist es immer wieder spannend, unterschiedliche Formen und die damit zu erzielenden Effekte zu testen.

Meine zuletzt fertiggestellte Pergola heißt Parapluie – Regenschirm. Das französische Wort Parapluie bedeutet buchstäblich »Schutz gegen Regen«, also genau gesagt wieder ein »shelter«, ganz nah am Körper, der einen zumindest den Oberkörper schützenden Raum schafft und der Möglichkeit zum Ausblick bietet. Mein Regenschirm schützt den Kopf vor dem Regen und vor der künstlichen Bewässerung, die sich ab und zu in Gang setzt, während die Füße von Sprühnebeln umspült werden. Er ist ein Grashügel auf Bronzebeinen, den man als eine Art Organismus oder ein ungewöhnliches, überwachsendes Gebäude ansehen kann.

Die Weiterentwicklung des Parapluie führt im Moment zu neuen bewachsenen Strukturen auf Stelzen: Pergolen als Denkmäler von Landschaft; Fragmente von wogenden Grasflächen, Feldern oder Hügeln, die auf dünnen Stützen ruhen; Installationen die über einen Platz wandern, die miteinander in Wechselbeziehung tretend über der Oberfläche schweben; kleine Dächer, die nachts Räume aus Licht bilden oder unter denen man einfach nur Schutz findet. Diese neuen Gebilde, eine Art Gratwanderung zwischen Bauwerk und gebauter Landschaft, werden im städtischen Raum eine Grenzzone zwischen Grasflächen und Bäumen besetzen. Sie werden mit den Baumkronen interferieren und diese in das offene Gelände verlängern.

Die eigentümliche Regenschirm-Pergola »Parapluie« besteht aus einem Grasdach auf Bronzestelzen. Bei Regen bleibt der Kopf der Schutzsuchenden zwar trocken, die Sprinkleranlage sorgt jedoch für erfrischende Fuß-Duschen.

The strange umbrella-pergola "Parapluie" consists of a grass roof on bronze stilts. While the head of someone seeking shelter is protected against the rain, the feet enjoy a refreshing shower provided by the sprinkler system.

Vergessene Tempel

Forgotten temples

Guido Hager

Woran denken Sie, wenn Sie sich einen Pavillon vorstellen? Ist es der kleine Holzbau im Schrebergarten oder das neue Modell aus dem Gartencenterkatalog? Ist er aus Stein, Holz oder Metall? Ist die Konstruktion offen – oder ist das bereits eine Laube, oder ist sie geschlossen – aber ist es dann nicht schon ein Haus? Mein erster Gedanke geht nach Tivoli, zum Tempel der Sibylle. Noch die Ruine zeugt von einem eleganten Bau mit korinthischen Säulen und verziertem Gebälk. Seit dem 17. Jahrhundert war sie häufig Bildgegenstand, da sie durch ihre reizvolle Lage über den Wasserfällen des Flusses Aino imponiert. Die Darstellungen bauen auf den Gegensatz zwischen der wilden Natur und dem ehemals vollkommenen Rundbau, was die jeweilige Wirkung steigert. Der Rundtempel ist ein in der Antike eher selten angewandter Bautypus für Sakralbauten. Der heutige Tempel in Tivoli wurde im 2. Jahrhundert als Tempel der Sibylle neben einen älteren zur Verehrung von Vesta erbaut. Wie er da steht, was ihn so berühmt machte, hat mit jenem Begriff zu tun, den wir im allgemeinen als Geist des Ortes oder Genius Loci bezeichnen. Der Genius ist laut Definition von Jan Pieper »ursprünglich eine altrömische Vorstellung von der menschlichen Seele (...) Später wurde diese Vorstellung auf die Welt der Geister übertragen, von denen man glaubte, dass sie in Bäumen, Gewässer, Felsen etc. wohnten. So kommt es zur Idee (...), dass der Geist eines Ortes für dessen atmosphärische Qualität verantwortlich sei. Hierauf gründet der auf das 18. Jahrhundert zurückgehende moderne Sprachgebrauch.«

Nach Duden ist ein Pavillon ein »frei stehender, kleiner, offener, meist runder Bau in einem Park«: genau so wie in Tivoli. Sprachgeschichtlich hat Pavillon keine klare Bedeutung. Ein Bezug wird zum zeltartigen Charakter von aufgespannten Flügeln bei Schmetterlingen mit dem (spät-)lateinischen *pāpilio* angeführt. Die ersten Zeugnisse der Gartenkunst zeigen bereits Pavillons, so ein Gemälde aus dem Grabe eines Heerführers aus Theben von Amenophis III um 1500 vor Christus im Zentrum des quadratischen Gartens einen Weingarten, umgeben von symmetrisch angeordneten Obstgärten, Dattelhainen sowie Wasserbecken und Pavillons, gefasst von einer hohen Mauer. Die umfassende Baumreihe erhöht den Eindruck der Abgeschlossenheit.

Im 1467 und 1499 gedruckten Romanwerk von Francesco Colonna, »Hypnerotomachia

What comes to your mind when you think of a pavilion? Is it a small wooden construction in an allotment or is it the latest model from the garden centre catalogue? Is it made of stone, wood or metal? Is it an open construction – or is that already considered an arbour? Or is it closed – but isn't it then already considered a house? The first thought that comes to my mind is the Temple of the Sibyl in Tivoli. The ruins of the temple still show evidence of the elegant construction with Corinthian pillars and ornamented entablature. Since the 17th century, it has often been used as a motif in paintings due to its impressive location above the waterfalls. The portrayals draw upon the contrast between untamed nature and the formerly perfectly shaped rotunda, with one intensifying the effect of the other.

In Classical Antiquity, the rotunda is a type of construction seldom implemented for sacred buildings. Today's temple in Tivoli was built in the 2nd century as the Temple of the Sibyl, right next to an older one built for the worship of Vesta. Its location, what made it so famous has something to do with the term we generally call "spirit of place" or Genius Loci. According to the definition of Jan Pieper, the Genius is "originally an idea of the human soul in ancient Rome (...). Later this idea was transferred to the world of spirits, believing they lived in trees, lakes, rivers and rocks etc.. Thus the idea evolved (...) that the spirit of a place was responsible for its atmospheric quality. Modern linguistic usage is based on this, having its roots in the 18th century.

According to the German dictionary Duden, a pavilion is "a freestanding, small, open and mostly round construction in a park" – just as in Tivoli. The linguistic history does not pro-

Pavillons – ein bis heute immer wieder verwendetes Motiv in der Geschichte von Architektur und Gartenkunst.

Pavilions – a motif that has been used in the history of architecture and landscape architecture over and over again until today.

vide a clear definition for the term pavilion. A relation to the tent-like character of the spread-out wings of a butterfly and the (late) Latin word *pāpilio* is mentioned.

The first evidence of landscape architecture already show existing pavilions, such as for example the painting found in the tomb of a Theben army commander of Amenophis III from 1500 B.C. In the centre of the square-shaped garden lies a vineyard, surrounded by symmetrically laid-out orchards, with date groves as well as ponds and pavilions and surrounded by a high wall. The trees lining the garden increase the impression of isloation.

In the novel "Hypnerotomachia Poliphili" by Francesco Colonna, printed in 1467 and 1499, the description of the hero's unfulfilled dream is translated into architecture by means of woodcuts. Poliphili is the hero of the novel who has fallen in love with Polia. During the – dreamed up – union with Polia, cupid takes him to Kythera, to the Island of Venus, in a barque. On the island, they pass through the concentrically laid-out gardens in a triumph wagon to unify in the central court framed by colonnades. The comparison to the "paradise on earth" in Dante's "Purgatory" suggests itself. He, too, as the narrator, lets Beatrice lead him to the circular "purgatorium" after being through hell and purgatory.

Here as there, as well as with Plinius, the place of lust is described as a rotunda encircled by colonnades. The maze-like island garden of Armida, where the crusaders Carlo and Ubaldo must free the imprisoned Rinaldo, is described as being circular as well. It is only with its destruction that Rinaldo gains his freedom. Both narratives imply that the enchanted garden, the paradise beyond

Poliphili«, wird die Beschreibung des unerfüllten Traumes des Helden mit Holzschnitten in Architektur umgesetzt. Der Romanheld Poliphili, der sich in Polia verliebt hat, wird in der – geträumten – Vereinigung mit seiner Angebeteten von Amor in einer Barke nach Kythera, zur Insel der Venus, übergesetzt. Dort durchfahren sie in einem Triumphwagen die konzentrisch aufgebauten Gärten um sich im zentralen, von Kolonnaden umstellten Platz zu vereinigen.

Der Vergleich zum »Irdischen Paradies« in Dantes »Purgatorio« liegt nahe. Auch er lässt sich als Ich-Erzähler nach Hölle und Fegefeuer ins kreisrunde Purgatorium von Beatrice leiten. Hier wie dort, aber auch bei Plinius wird der Lustort als eine kreisrunde, durch Säulenhallen gefasste Fläche beschrieben. Ebenso kreisförmig wird der zentrale Lustort im labyrinthischen Inselgarten der Armida beschrieben, wo die Kreuzritter Carlo und Ubaldo den gefangenen Rinaldo befreien müssen. Rinaldo wird erst mit dessen Zerstörung befreit. Beide Erzählungen legen nahe, dass der verwunschene Garten, das unerreichbare Para-

dies, von Venus oder einer Hexe regiert wird, sich auf einer Insel befindet oder mindestens an einem unerreichbaren wilden Ort und dass an der Kreisform festgehalten wird.

Die Renaissancegärten zeigen alle jene Kleinarchitekturen, wie sie bei Collona abgebildet waren: In Italien und im Norden der Alpen weinberankte Pergolen, Kühle spendende Grotten und Nymphäen, ein- und zweigeschossige begrünte Gartenhäuser und Steinhäuser mit oder ohne Loggien, wie uns das Abbildungen bei Falda der römischen Gärten, oder um 1600 Giusto Utens der florentinischen Gärten, oder de Vries der holländischen Gartenkunst zeigen. Der Typus des Rundtempels war zu dieser Zeit omnipräsent.

Claude Lorrain (1600–1682) hat nachhaltig mit seiner Malerei das später zum Topos gewordene Bild von Tivoli geprägt, die römische Campagna als Heimat Arkadiens bestimmt und den Sibyllentempel als Zitat in

Der Tempel der Sibylle gilt als Urform des Pavillons. Der Rundbau inspirierte aufgrund seiner vollendeten Form und seiner spektakulären Lage über den Wasserfällen des Flusses Aino viele Künstler, unter anderem Giovanni Battista Piranesi (1720–1778), von dem der abgebildete Stich stammt.

The Temple of the Sibyl is considered the prototype of the pavilion. The rotunda with its perfect form and impressive location above the waterfalls of Aino River inspired many artists, among them Giovanni Battista Piranesi (1720–1778) whose engraving is shown in the photo.

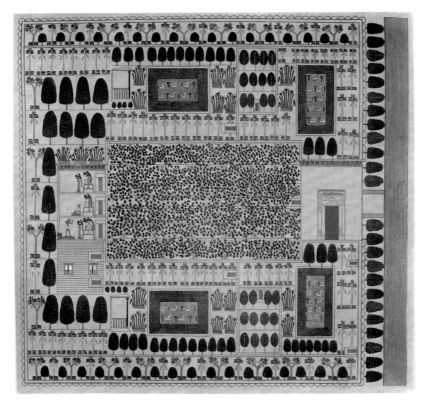

reach, reigned by a witch or by Venus, is located on an island or in an isolated, far-off place in the wilderness, its shape being circular as well.

The Renaissance gardens show all the small structures as shown in Colonna's work: in Italy and in the north of the Alps, cooling grottos and nymphaeums, pergolas entwined with vines, one- and two-storey garden houses covered with greenery, stone houses with or without loggias as shown in the painting of Roman gardens by Fal-da, Florentine gardens by Giusto Utens (around 1600), or the Dutch landscape architecture by de Vries. The rotunda was omnipresent.

With his paintings, the artist Claude Lorrain (1600–1682) has lastingly shaped the image of Tivoli which later became a topos – a traditional theme; he has defined the Roman Campagna as home of Arcadia and caused the Sibylline Temple as a quote to become pars pro toto in the reception of his work.

The paintings of Lorrain were collected by Ludwig XIV (1638–1715), although his gardens lacked this kind of scenery. Though, in his self-portrait as Apollo, the sun god, he was highly familiar with Classical Antiquity. In his garden designed by André Le Nôtre, as well as in Vaux-le-Vicomte, there were hardly any pavilions. The Grotto of Thetis or the orangery should be viewed as a continuation of the castle, and the buildings surrounding the Petit or Grand Trianon were constructions each with its very own character. In Versailles, however, the boscage "La Colonnade" resembles very much the literary topos of the central places of lust as the ones on the islands of Armida or on Kythera.

Other baroque castle gardens knew pavilions as an independent form of construction – as for

der Rezeption seines Werkes zum pars pro toto werden lassen. Die Bilder von Lorrain wurden von Ludwig XIV (1638–1715) gesammelt, obwohl seine Gärten den Reiz einer solchen Szenerie nicht kannten. Dafür war er in seiner Selbstdarstellung als Apollo, dem Sonnengott, mit der Antike aufs Beste vertraut. In seinem Garten, gestaltet von André Le Nôtre, gab es, wie zuvor in Vaux-le-Vicomte, kaum Pavillons. Die Thetis-Grotte oder die Orangerie sind noch als Fortsetzung des Schlosses zu lesen, Und die Gebäude um das Petit oder Grand Trianon waren Schlossanlagen eigener Prägung. In Versailles erinnert das Boskett »La Colonnade« aber sehr an den literarischen Topos der zentralen Lustorte wie jener auf der Inseln der Armida oder auf Kythera. Andere barocke Schlossgärten kannten eigenständige Pavillons wie die beiden im Großen Garten von Hannover-Her-

example the two pavilions constructed by Remy de la Fosse in the Great Gardens of Hannover-Herrenhausen in 1707/08 and located along the canal as a focal point for the "Lindenalleen". Pavilions and gloriettes were often the focal point in the central axis of a baroque castle.

In England in the early 18th century, a garden type with an irregular layout was developed, mirroring the open country side: with its buildings and monuments seemingly placed at random, very specific kinds of sentimental values are being expressed:

Artificial ruins bring the past to mind, hermitages express solitude, a barn house renders simplicity, Chinese pavilions invoke the exotic and temples represent classical magnitude.

In the landscape garden, the Sibyl Temple appeared in Stowe in 1734 for the first time: Different variations of the temple have since graced many gardens in England and on the Continent – always in the original intact form. As a ruin it first appeared in the garden of Ermenonville in 1776/77. With the "Temple of Modern Philosophy" in Ermenonville, Hubert Robert has probably created the most impressive image of the entire site, allowing the observer to have the strongest association with the original. It is located above a waterfall and rises above a surface of water surrounding the small island with Rousseau's grave. Robert stayed in Tivoli between 1760 and 1763. There, he often drew and painted the Temple of the Sibyl as well as citing it in Capricci.

The Venus Temple in Wörlitz has existed since 1774. According to Ludwig Trauzettel, this wooden rotunda represents the earliest replica of the Sibyl temple in Germany.

renhausen 1707/1708 als Blickpunkt der Lindenalleen entlang der Graft aufgestellten Pavillons von Remy de la Fosse. Oft bildeten Pavillons oder Glorietten den Blickpunkt in der Hauptachse eines barocken Schlosses.

Mit dem im frühen 18. Jahrhundert in England entwickelten unregelmäßigen, der freien Natur nachgebildeten Gartentypus werden durch scheinbar zufällige Bauten und Denkmäler ganz bestimmte Gefühlswerte ausgedrückt: Mit künstlichen Ruinen wird die Vergangenheit beschworen, Eremitagen drücken Einsamkeit aus, ein Bauernhaus Schlichtheit, chinesische Pavillons das Exotische, und Tempel versinnbildlichen antike Größe. Im Landschaftsgarten erschien der Tempel der Sibylle zum ersten Mal im Jahre 1734 in Stowe. Seitdem ziert der Tempel in verschiedenen Ausprägungen, immer zum intakten Bauwerk rekonstruiert, viele Gärten

In seinem Bild »Landschaft: Komposition in Tivoli« von 1870 beschreibt William Turner in warmen Farben die morgendliche Stimmung in Tivoli. Über der Landschaftskomposition prangt majestätisch der Rundtempel der Sibylle.

In his painting "Landscape: Composition of Tivoli" from 1870 William Turner describes the morning mood in Tivoli in warm colours. The Temple of the Sibyl sits enthroned above the lovely landscape setting.

Englands und des Kontinents. Als Ruine erschien er erstmals, zwischen 1776 und 1777 erbaut, im Garten von Ermenonville. In Ermenonville hat Hubert Robert vermutlich das eindrucksvollste und assoziationsreichste Bild der gesamtem Anlage geschaffen – mit dem »Tempel der modernen Philosophie«. Er steht über einem Wasserfall und einer Wasserfläche mit dem Inselgrab von Rousseau. Robert weilte zwischen 1760 und

In his "Theory of Garden Art", Hirschfeld describes in 1780 the landscape garden in Hohenheim near Stuttgart in great detail. Herein, he also mentions, that "these ruins are the greatest form of reproduction that one can imagine. With its great, magnificent, and picturesque waterfall they

represent a copy of the famous scenery in Tivoli."
On June 16, 1787, Johann Wolfgang Goethe
wrote in his "Italian Journey": "In Tivoli, I was
very tired from walking and drawing in the heat.
(..) I don't want to say any further. This, again,
is a high point of earthly matters."

1763 in Tivoli. Er hat dort den Tempel der Sibylle häufig gezeichnet und
gemalt und in Capricci zitiert. In Wörlitz steht seit 1774 der Venustem-
pel, eine hölzerne Rotunde, die gemäß Ludwig Trauzettel den frühesten
in Deutschland nachgebauten Sibyllentempel von Tivoli darstellt.
Hirschfeld beschreibt in seiner »Theorie der Gartenkunst« von 1780 aus-
führlich die englischen Anlagen in Hohenheim bei Stuttgart. Darin er-

wähnt er auch »diese Ruinen sind das Herrlichste, was man sich in dieser Art von Nachahmung denken kann. Sie stellen mit ihrem großen, prächtigen und malerischen Wasserfall eine Nachbildung von der berühmten Scene zu Tivoli dar.« Am 16. Juni 1787 beschreibt Johann Wolfgang Goethe in seiner »Italienischen Reise«: »In Tivoli war ich sehr müde vom Spazierengehen und vom Zeichnen in der Hitze. (...) Weiter mag ich gar nichts sagen. Das ist wieder ein Gipfel irdischer Dinge.«

Das spätere 19. und frühe 20. Jahrhundert kennt jede Art von Pavillons. Sie sind wohl noch als Blickfang konzipiert, dienen aber nützlichen Belangen. 1902 schreibt Thomas Mawson: »Der Architektonische Garten ist unvollständig ohne Gartenhaus.« Gertrude Jekyll fordert, dass ein Gartenhaus behaglich und praktisch sein soll. Auch Mader, Verfasser des 1992 erschienenen Buches »Der Architektonische Garten in England«, geht zuerst auf praktische Belange wie die Gefahr von Staub und Spinnweben ein. Weiter unten wird aber der wertvolle Hinweis zu den Loggie delle Muse der Villa Lante gegeben und dass man im Gartenhaus den Musen näher stehe. Meier/Ries heben in ihrem Standardwerk zur Gartenkunst von 1904 hervor, »für mythologische und symbolische Tempel (...) schwärmt heute niemand, so dass sie hier außer Betracht bleiben können.«

Im Ausstellungskatalog »Modern Gardens and Landscape« des Museum of Modern Art, New York von 1964 (1986) findet sich kein einziger Gartenpavillon. Im vielleicht schönsten Beispiel, dem Plaza del Bebedero de los Caballos von Luis Barragán, erbaut zwischen 1958 und 1962, hat sich der Pavillon in eine Wasserfläche, in weiße und blaue freistehende Mauern verselbständigt.

Den traditionellen Faden nimmt Ian Hamilton Finlay seit 1966 in seinem eigenen Garten und in seinem künstlerischen Werk auf. Ihm geht es in den Szenerien seines »Little Sparta« um die Bezüge zur klassischen Gartenkunst, um die »Sichtbarmachung von Bildern, die kulturell verankert im Kopf des Betrachters präsent sind und sein Denken und Handeln beeinflussen.« Er hinterfragt aber auch die »schönen« und »guten« Bilder der Landschaftsgärten, indem ein Landschaftsgemälde zum Tarnanstrich eines Panzers wird, die krönenden Abschlüsse eines Tores zwei steinerne Handgranaten zeigen oder eine in Stein gemeißelte Sandsteinplatte mit der Aufschrift »Et in Arcadia Ego – After Nicolas Poussin« einen Panzer in einer Landschaft zeigt. Als er zum Aufstellen einiger vor der Witterung zu schützenden Arbeiten einen Stall benutzen möchte und

The late 19th and early 20th century knows all forms of pavilions. They are still designed as a focal point but have functional meaning. In 1902, Thomas Mawson writes: "The architectural garden is not complete without a summer-house." Gertrude Jekyll demands that a summer-house should be practical and comfortable. Mader, author of the book: "The architectural garden in England" first discusses the questions of practicality as e.g. the danger of dust and spider webs. Later on, however, he gives valuable information on the Loggie delle Muse of the Villa Lante and that in summer-houses one is closer to the muses. In their standard work on landscape architecture from 1904, Meier/Ries emphasize that "nowadays, no one favours mythological and symbolical temples due to which they can be neglected."

In the catalogue of the 1964 (1986) exhibition "Modern Gardens and Landscape" of the MOMA in New York, not a single garden pavilion can be found. In perhaps the most beautiful example – the Plaza del Bebedero de los Caballos of Luis Barragán (1958–62) – the pavilion underwent a transformation into a water surface, into freestanding, white and blue walls. Since 1966 Ian Hamilton Finlay has taken up tradition in his own garden and the artwork. The sceneries of his work "Little Sparta" focus on the relations to the classical landscape architecture, to "show images that are present and culturally embedded in the viewers mind and affect his thinking and acting." He also analyses the "pretty" and "good" images of the landscape gardens, whereby a landscape painting becomes the camouflage paint on a tank, two stone hand grenades represent the final touch on a gate or a sandstone plate with the inscription reading: "Et in Arcadia Ego – After Nicolas Poussin" shows a tank in the open country side.

When he wanted to use a stable to protect some of his art work from wind and weather during erection, yet did not want to dub it "art gallery" because this term is too closely related to profit, his appeal submitted for the "Garden Temple" – the stable with demi-columns, capitals and inscriptions – was not granted, because the term couldn't be found in the computer. A part of Finlay's work of art is directed against this very ignorance.

In the graveyard Fürstenwald near Chur (1992–1996), Dieter Kienast and Günther Vogt chose a high supporting wall to close the view-exposed side of the burial plots, the three other sides being surrounded by trees. Located on one side of the wall is the entrance and the chapel with the funeral parlour, while on the other side a simple concrete construction marks the place. "Slowly, the remembrance of those who passed away blends with the sensuous perception of the presence of landscape and nature", so Kienast's intent. Wall and pavilion become a landscape symbol. Kienast and Vogt built a similar pavilion for a private garden. "On the eastern side, a path zigzags to the pavilion with a splendid view, located at the highest point of the garden. (...) Curiosity drives us to the pavilion, slightly hidden behind bushes with an inedible letter-balustrade. (...) The framed image is loaded with meaning: Far back, in the haze the Alps – directly in front of us the city with the highest church tower in Europe, the plants of the garden and "Ogni pensiero vola". The image seems modern and antiquated

diesen aber nicht Galerie nennt, da der Begriff mit Profit besetzt ist, wird ihm die Bewilligung für den eingereichten »Garden Temple«, den mit Halbsäulen, Kapitellen und Inschriften versehenen Stall, nicht erteilt, weil der Begriff im Computer fehlt. Gegen diese Ignoranz wendet sich ein Teil des Werkes von Finlay.

Dieter Kienast und Günther Vogt haben im Friedhof Fürstenwald bei Chur (1992–96) die auf drei Seiten von Wald gefassten Grabstellen zur Aussichtslage hin mit einer hohen Stützmauer abgeschlossen, an der sich der Eingang und die Kapelle mit Aufbahrungsraum auf der einen Seite befindet, auf der anderen Seite aber eine einfache Betonkonstruktion den Ort auszeichnet. »Langsam vermischt sich das Gedenken an den Verstorbenen mit dem sinnlichen Wahrnehmen der Gegenwärtigkeit von Landschaft und Natur«, so Kienasts Absicht. Mauer und Pavillon werden zum Landschaftszeichen. Einen ähnlichen Pavillon haben Kienast und Vogt für einen Privatgarten gebaut. »Auf der Ostseite führt ein Zickzackweg zum Aussichtspavillon am höchsten Punkt des Gartens. (...) Ziel der Neugierde ist der oben im Gebüsch leicht versteckte Pavillon mit seiner nicht lesbaren Buchstabenbrüstung. (...) Das gerahmte Bild ist mit Bedeutung aufgeladen: ganz hinten im Dunst die Alpen, die Stadt mit dem höchsten Kirchturm von Europa, die Pflanzen des Gartens und direkt vor uns »Ogni pensiero vola«. Das Bild wirkt gleichzeitig modern und antiquiert. Es verkörpert das Credo visueller Kommunikation, die Gleichwertigkeit von Wort und Bild, erinnert uns aber auch an die Sinnsprüche in alten Gärten«, so Kienast.

Zu guter Letzt gehe ich auf meine 1988 geplante und 1994 fertiggestellte Außenanlage für die Telecom in der Lehmgrube Binz in Zürich ein (siehe *Topos 12*). Der zentrale Pavillon liegt als traditionelles Element der Gartenarchitektur im Brennpunkt der Anlage und spielt als elementare Kleinarchitektur mit dem Licht. Das Artefakt und die Natur treten in eine sich gegenseitig durchdringende Beziehung: Die Natur braucht den Betrachter, um als Natur erkannt zu werden.

Mein Pavillon steht in der langen Kette von Entwicklungsstadien vom griechischen Tempel zur durchbrochenen Form. Das Zitat ist nicht direkt: Der Pavillon weist keine korinthischen Säulen auf. Aber er steht in einem Naturraum und schwebt über einer Kaskade. Der Wunsch, eine vollkommene Form in die natürliche Landschaft zu setzen, diesen sich ergänzenden Gegensatz zu konstruieren, war beim Entwurf leitend. Und nicht nur bei meinem. Der Faden der Tradition wird wieder verstärkt

at the same time. It represents the credo of visual communication, the equality of word and image, but also reminds us of the epigrams in old gardens."

At last, let me focus on one of my projects, planned in 1988 and completed in 1994 – the Telekom complex in the loam pit in Zurich (see *Topos 12*). As the traditional element of garden architecture the central pavilion is the focus of the site and – as a small, basic architectural structure – plays with light.

Artefact and nature come together and form a reciprocally penetrating relationship: Nature needs the observer to be conceived as nature. My pavilion stands in the long line of stages of development – from the Greek temple to the open-work construction. This is no direct quote: The pavilion has no Corinthian columns. But it is located in a space of nature, hovering over a cascade.

The wish to place a perfect shape into the natural landscape, to engineer this complementing contrast was the central idea for the design. And not only with my design. More and more the trend turns toward tradition again. Placing a small architectural structure into the landscape should not just serve one single purpose but should try to express the spirit of a place.

The pavilion uses the theme of interplay between focal point and outlook, between observer and the things to be observed in an almost ideal form. It is located in the range of association. We must know the roots of our images. Designing a reference to the Temple of the Sibyl is not a new idea, but still an exciting one. Who knows which spirits we awaken with our actions?

aufgenommen. Die Setzung einer Kleinarchitektur in einen Landschaftsraum soll nicht mehr einem Zweck dienen, sondern versucht, den Geist des Ortes auszudrücken. Der Pavillon thematisiert geradezu ideal das Spiel zwischen Blickfang und Ausblick, zwischen Betrachter und zu Betrachtendem. Er steht im Bereich der Assoziation. Wir müssen wissen, woher unsere Bilder stammen. Eine Referenz an den Tempel der Sibylle zu gestalten ist zwar nicht neu, aber immer noch aufregend. Wer weiß, welche Geister wir damit wecken.

Mittelpunkt der nach einem Entwurf von Guido Hager 1994 fertiggestellten Außenanlage des Telecomgebäudes in Zürich Binz ist ein kreisrunder Pavillon. Inspirationsquelle war auch hier der Tempel der Sibylle.

A circular pavilion is the focal point of the Telekom complex in Zurich-Binz, completed in 1994 and constructed according to Guido Hager's plans. Here again, the Temple of the Sibyl was the source of inspiration.

Authors

Anneke Bokern, who was born in 1971, studied art history and English literature at the Free University of Berlin. She has been living in Amsterdam since 2000, working as a freelance journalist.

Paolo L. Bürgi is adjunct professor of landscape architecture at the University of Pennsylvania and visiting professor at the Università degli Studi di Reggio Calabria, Italy. After graduating in landscape architecture and planning at the Engineering School of Rapperswil in 1975, he began practicing as a freelance landscape architect in 1977, when he opened his own practice in Camorino, Switzerland.

Andre Dekker, who was born in 1956, is an artist. In 1993 he founded the Observatorium group together with Geert van de Camp and Ruud Reutelingsperger.

Monika Gora was born in 1959. She studied landscape architecture at the Swedish University of Agriculture in Uppsala and Alnarp. In 1989 she set up her own practice, Gora art&landscape, working both as a landscape architect and artist.

Guido Hager was born in 1958. After being apprenticed as a gardener and florist, he studied landscape architecture at the Interkantonale Technikum (Engineering School) in Rapperswil. He has had his own landscape architecture office in Zurich since 1984.

Vesa Honkonen, born in 1958, has his own architecture office in Helsinki Finland. His projects have included architecture and urban, lighting, and interior design.

Paul Kersten, born in 1966, graduated in garden and landscape design from the International Agricultural University of Larenstein in 1991 and gained his degree in landscape architecture in 1999. He worked for municipalities and, since 1997, he has been senior landscape architect at the VHP office of urban planners, architects and landscape architects in Rotterdam.

Margit Klammer, born in 1958, completed her studies at the University of Applied Arts in Vienna in 1983, and has been living and working as a freelance artist in Meran ever since. Many of her projects were developed in collaboration with Wolfram H. Pardatscher PVC Architects and Partners, also of Meran.

Nikolaus Knebel, born in 1972, studied architecture in Berlin, Delft and Singapore between 1992 and 1998. In 1996 he worked for OMA, in 1999 for Toyo Ito in Tokyo, and in 2001 at the Bauhaus Foundation, Dessau. He has been a free-lance architect in Berlin since 2000.

Kirstine Laukli, born in 1970, studied landscape architecture at the Norwegian Agricultural University from 1989 to 1994, and has been working for the Norwegian road construction office in Buskerud ever since.

Roy Mänttäri, born in 1955, graduated from Helsinki University of Technology in 1986. He has been a member of the Finnish Association of Architects (SAFA) since1986 and has run his own office since 1989. He became the head of the exhibition department at the Museum of Finnish Architecture in 2003.

Regina Schineis was born in 1966. After completing her studies in church music, she studied architecture from 1989 to 1996 at the Technical University in Darmstadt. From 1998 to 2000 she was a teaching and research assistant at the chair of architectural construction at the Technical University in Munich. She founded her own architecture practice in Augsburg in 1998.

Thies Schröder, born in 1965, studied landscape planning at the Technical University in Berlin and worked at the Institute of Landscape Economics. He has worked as a free-lance journalist since 1989.

Olga Gudrún Sigfúsdóttir, born in 1969, studied architecture at the Technical University of Berlin from 1992 to 2000. Her diploma thesis was on baths ("Badelust"). She has been working for VA Architects in Reykjavik since 2003.

Axel Simon, born in 1966, studied architecture in Düsseldorf and Berlin and architectural history and theory in Zurich. He works as a teaching and research assistant at the Swiss Federal Institute of Technology in Zurich (ETH) and as an architecture critic for the Swiss daily *Tages-Anzeiger.*

Frank R. Werner, born in 1944, graduated in architecture from the University of Stuttgart in 1972. Since 1993 he has been head of the Institute of Architectural History and Theory (AGT) at Wuppertal University. He has been a visiting professor at several universities and has published many books and articles on 20th-century architectural history and theory.

Erik Wessel, born in 1940, studied at the State Academy of Art in Oslo from 1961 to 1969. He teaches in Trondheim, Ås and at the Institute of Colour.

Barbara Wiskemann, born in 1971, is an architect living in Zurich. She is a teaching and research assistant for Professor Andrea Deplazes at the ETH in Zurich.

Photo credits

Robert Schäfer: 7
Frank R. Werner: 8, 9
Computersimulation des
Department of Architecture am M.I.T., Camebridge/Mass., aus: Russell
Ferguson (Ed.): At The
End Of The Century,
Hatje-Cantz, Ostfildern
1999, Seite 43: 10
Entwurf Natan Altman,
Reproduktion, aus:
Vladimir Tolstoy, Irina
Bibikova, Catherine
Cooke: Street Art Of The
Revolution, Thames und
Hudson, London 1990,
Seite 89: 11
Haus-Rucker-Co, aus:
Heinrich Klotz (Hrsg.),
Haus-Rucker-Co 1967 bis
1983, Vieweg, Braunschweig/Wiesbaden,
1984, Seite 147: 12
Gert van der Vlugt, aus:
Frank Werner, Covering +
Exposing, Die Architektur
von Coop Himmelb(l)au,
Birkhäuser, Basel 2000,
Seite 35 : 13 top
Anonym, aus: Architectural Design Profile No.
87, London 1990, Seite
42 : 13 bottom
Eckhart Matthäus: 15 (3),
16 (2), 17, 18 (2), 19 (3)
Observatorium: 22, 23
top, bottom right and
centre, 25
Harry Cock: 23 bot. left
Hans Pattist: 26, 27, 28,
30 second from top, bottom, 31 (2)
Panoramafoto L.H.
Duhen, Amsterdam 2002:
29, 30 top, third from top
Giosanna Crivelli: 38 (2),
39, 42 top, 43
Paolo Bürgi: 42 bottom
Tacsi Keresztes: 45, 46
Arup: 48, 49
Alexander Moers: 50 top
Toerisme Brugge: 50 bottom, 51
Rien Korteknie: 53
Korteknie Stuhlmacher
Architecten (KSAR): 54
(2), 55
Christoph Seyferth: 56 top
Büro OI: 56 bottom
Michael Rakowitz: 57
Peter Tillessen: 58, 60
Roman Mensing / artdoc.de: 59
Anne Garde: 62 (3, except
top)
Robert Latour d'Affaure:
62 top
Vrbica & Tošović: 63 (2)
Office Services Barbara
Imesch (OSBI): 65 (4)
Olga Gudrún Sigfússdóttir: 68 (2), 70 (2), 71
Icelandic Tourist Board
2001/Photo: Haukur
Snorrason: 69
Jussi Tiainen: 74 (2), 75
Rauno Träskelin: 76 (2), 77
Roy Mänttäri: 78
Vesa Honkonen Architects: 80 (3), 81 (2)
84 top and centre
Statens vegvesen: 84 (3)
Jan Indrehus: 85
Monika Gora: 88, 89 (2),
92 (2), 93
Giovanni Battista Piranesi,
Kunstantiquariat Monika
Schmidt, München: 95
Ägyptischer Plan, aus:
Virgilio Vercelloni, European Gardens. Milano
1990, Plate 3: 96
William Turner. Landschaft: Komposition in
Tivoli, 1817, Privatbesitz,
aus: William Turner, Licht
und Farbe. DuMont
Buchverlag, Köln 2001. S.
157: 97
Christian Vogt: 98/99
Guido Hager: 101

Translations

German/English:
Almuth Seebohm: 4, 21,
103
Valerie Mader: 6, 26, 32,
47, 52, 58, 87, 94
Judith Harrison: 15, 37,
44, 66, 83
Dutch/German:
Beate Rupprecht: 26
Regina Sasse: 21
English/German:
Peter Zöch: 73, 79
Norwegian/German:
Robert Schäfer: 83

Impressum

This book also exists as
the magazine Topos – European Landscape Magazine at Callwey Publishers
(ISBN 3-7667-1588-7).

Translation from German
into English: Judith Harrison, Valerie Mader, Almuth Seebohm
Graphic Design: Heike
Frese-Pieper, Sabine Hoffmann

A CIP catalogue record
for this book is available
from the Library of Congress, Washington D.C.,
USA

Bibliographic information
published by Die
Deutsche Bibliothek
Die Deutsche Bibliothek
lists this publication in the
Deutsche Nationalbibliografie; detailed bibliographic data is available in
the internet at
http://dnb.ddb.de.

© 2004 Birkhäuser –
Publishers for Architecture,
P.O. Box 133, CH-4010
Basel, Switzerland
Part of Springer Science +
Business Media

Verlag Georg D. W. Callwey GmbH & Co. KG,
Munich

Printed on acid-free paper
produced from chlorinefree pulp. TCF ∞

Printed in Germany

ISBN 3-7643-6980-9

987654321

www.birkhauser.ch
www.topos.de